# REASONABLE Rx

# REASONABLE Rx

## Solving the Drug Price Crisis

Stan Finkelstein      Peter Temin

Vice President, Publisher: Tim Moore
Associate Publisher and Director of Marketing: Amy Neidlinger
Acquisitions Editor: Martha Cooley
Editorial Assistant: Pamela Boland
Development Editor: Russ Hall
Digital Marketing Manager: Julie Phifer
Marketing Coordinator: Megan Colvin
Cover Designer: John Barnett
Managing Editor: Gina Kanouse
Project Editor: Jovana San Nicolas-Shirley
Copy Editor: Carol Pogoni
Proofreader: Lisa Stumpf
Senior Indexer: Cheryl Lenser
Compositor: ICC Macmillan Inc.
Manufacturing Buyer: Dan Uhrig

© 2008 by Pearson Education, Inc.
Publishing as FT Press
Upper Saddle River, New Jersey 07458

FT Press offers excellent discounts on this book when ordered in quantity for bulk purchases or special sales. For more information, please contact U.S. Corporate and Government Sales, 1-800-382-3419, corpsales@pearsontechgroup.com. For sales outside the U.S., please contact International Sales at international@pearsoned.com.

Company and product names mentioned herein are the trademarks or registered trademarks of their respective owners.

Printed in the United States of America

First Printing: January 2008

ISBN-10: 0-13-234449-1
ISBN-13: 978-0-13-234449-4

Pearson Education LTD., London
Pearson Education Australia PTY, Limited.
Pearson Education Singapore, Pte. Ltd.
Pearson Education North Asia, Ltd.
Pearson Education Canada, Ltd.
Pearson Educatión de Mexico, S.A. de C.V.
Pearson Education—Japan
Pearson Education Malaysia, Pte. Ltd.

Library of Congress Cataloging-in-Publication Data

Finkelstein, Stan N.
  Reasonable Rx : how to lower drug prices / Stan N. Finkelstein, Peter Temin.
     p. ; cm.
  ISBN-13: 978-0-13-234449-4 (hardback : alk. paper)
  ISBN-10: 0-13-234449-1 (hardback : alk. paper)
  1. Drugs—Prices—United States.   2. Prescription pricing—United States.
  3. Pharmaceutical industry—United States.   I. Temin, Peter.   II. Title.
  HD9666.4.F55 2008
  338.4'361510973—dc22
                                                                    2007036128

*To Jill and Charlotte*

# CONTENTS

# ACKNOWLEDGMENTS

This book is one of many research products that grew out of a shared vision by Sloan Foundation President Ralph Gomory and our MIT colleagues, Thomas Allen and Charles Cooney, which led to the formation of the MIT Program on the Pharmaceutical Industry in 1991. Anthony Sinskey and Robert Rubin became prominent members of the team. Rubin, in particular, was the source of numerous insights and anecdotes about the field of medicine, some of which are reflected in this manuscript.

We are pleased to have brought our perspectives as a physician (Finkelstein) and an economist (Temin) to the multidisciplinary team. We continue to observe, through the window these perspectives create, the effects of dramatic changes that are unfolding in drug development and the pharmaceutical marketplace. We are grateful for everything we have learned from interacting with our colleagues over more than 17 years. We thank the Sloan Foundation for its major commitment to this activity over the entire period.

We also are grateful to MIT's Undergraduate Research Opportunities Program, in which MIT students get a taste for doing research. We thank Julia Dennett, Qinyuan Liu, Juan Prajogo, and Laila Shabir for their research assistance.

We thank Scott Cooper for his able editorial help with the writing of this book. And finally we thank Jeffrey Harris and Adam Sonnenschein for their comments on the completed manuscript.

# ABOUT THE AUTHORS

**Stan Finkelstein**, a physician and health policy specialist, is a Senior Research Scientist in the MIT Engineering Systems Division and the Harvard-MIT Division of Health Sciences and Technology. He co-directs the Sloan Foundation-chartered MIT Program on the Pharmaceutical Industry. Dr. Finkelstein also serves as Senior Lecturer in Harvard Medical School's Department of Health Care Policy, where he is a director of the MD/MBA degree program. In recognition of his broad experience and knowledge, he was selected as one of eighteen members of the original Model Guidelines Expert Committee of the United States Pharmacopeia, tasked with devising a framework for medicines to be covered under the new Medicare prescription drug benefit.

**Peter Temin**, a widely cited economist and economic historian, is the Elisha Gray II Professor of Economics and former head of the Economics Department at MIT. He is the author of several well-known industry studies, including the pioneering book *Taking Your Medicine: Drug Regulation in the United States*. He has written extensively about the interface between health care and corporate providers of health insurance in the United States. In addition to his research on health care and pharmaceuticals, Dr. Temin studies and is writing about current U.S. income distribution and the economics of ancient Rome.

# INTRODUCTION

The age of effective medicinal drugs, which dawned about 50 years ago, transformed the health care industry. Americans have become used to taking a pill to cure many diseases and improve their lives in other ways. Many senior citizens, though, can recall growing up in a world where there were no easy cures for many serious conditions that today are regarded as little more than irritations. President Calvin Coolidge's son died from an infection he picked up while playing in the White House rose garden. There's no reason anyone in America should face that risk today. But good drug therapies are only as good as patients' access to them. The best cures in the world are of no use if exorbitant prices put them out of reach.

It is no exaggeration to say that we are past being on the verge of a crisis. No one reading this book can honestly deny that the prices of drugs are high and are getting higher. Even for those fortunate enough to have health insurance that pays part of the cost of prescription drugs, the co-payments keep increasing and insurers put more and more restrictions on what therapies they'll cover. As a revolution in science and technology unfolds that brings us new drugs that are targeted almost to the individual patient, the magnitude of the crisis only grows.

In the not-too-distant future, perhaps just around the corner, we might be faced with the following scenario: new, more effective, "personalized" drugs that address small patient groups but are priced beyond what any individual can afford and what any insurer is willing to pay. If that happens, then the federal government will intervene to control prices—which the experiences of Europe and Canada have shown kills innovation.

What has gotten us to this point? The culprit is a broken system that we've let languish for too long without fixing. It's a flawed system that combines three components that all too often work against each other.

The first component is *money*. It costs a fortune to develop a new drug, but the potential profits are huge. Not unexpectedly, the pharmaceutical industry is driven to maximize those profits and firms are racing to develop the next big *blockbuster* drug that will bring in $1 billion or more in sales.

The second component is science. New scientific discoveries about how diseases work, coupled with new technologies, are leading to new therapies that work better for specific patients. We can even know in advance how likely the outcome of a therapy will be with a given patient. But that means selling a drug to smaller numbers of people. If a company's objective is blockbusters, this busts the business model.

The third component is *incentives*. Simply put, we have the wrong ones. The choices that research-driven pharmaceutical firms make today about which drugs to pursue in their discovery and development programs are just too far afield of what society needs most. For every slight variation on a blockbuster antihistamine for hay fever that the industry pursues, a pressing societal need gets ignored. The incentives, through no direct fault of the industry, are seriously askew.

No wonder we see so many instances where business decisions encroach on science. This is a situation that cannot stand. Some serious changes need to be made—before it's too late.

Lots of people are worried about this situation. Rising drug prices are increasing the cost of health insurance because drugs continue to grow as a share of overall health costs and insurance reimbursements. Those of us who have insurance worry that premiums will increase to the point where we can no longer afford our coverage. State governments that operate Medicaid are finding their costs rising so fast that it puts pressure to restrict the funds available for other purposes. And if all the estimates hold, the federal government, which operates Medicare, will find that the cost of the new Medicare Part D drug benefit to senior citizens is significantly larger than anticipated.

A spate of recent books by distinguished doctors and editors of the prestigious *New England Journal of Medicine* address these high drug prices and even recommend ways to lower them.[1] Our book is different, however. Here we propose a comprehensive solution that honors the tremendous innovation of the pharmaceutical industry, takes full advantage of today's scientific revolution, and speaks directly to how society can ensure we all get the drugs we need. In doing so, we aim directly at a profound misconception: that high drug prices are a prerequisite if we are to continue to make medical advances with pharmaceuticals. No, the real issue is risk—and who bears it.

Just as we rely on private industry to produce our clothes, houses, cars, and other things that enhance our lives, we rely on a private pharmaceutical industry to create our medicines. But don't be confused by the word "private;" the U.S. government has long been part of the process of drug discovery, manufacture, and sale. In fact, the government's involvement predates the revolution in drug therapies and goes back to the beginning of the twentieth century. And since it's both a private and government effort today, it stands to reason that any solution to the crisis we've described should also be public and private. That solution begins with risk.

Americans face a lot of risks in their lives. In the United States, people accept risks in order to obtain the potential rewards. Even if the economy doesn't always work as it's supposed to, it's designed to allow you to choose your education and career. It is structured for business enterprises to choose where and how they produce their products. True, some government constraints exist in the form of rules and standards, sometimes called "regulations." After all, you couldn't drive your car safely down the street if we didn't have a rule about driving on the right-hand side. The price to pay for successful management of many risks is having rules and behaving in common with other people.

In the world of finance, risk is rampant, and the government plays a big part in making sure things run well. For instance, you can invest in companies with the assurance that they will honor their contracts with you because of government regulations. The government participates in the risk of investing in many other ways, too. Take bankruptcy, a way to limit the cost of unsuccessful gambles. No one wants to declare bankruptcy, but it reduces the losses that will be incurred if a risky enterprise fails. It eases the cost of risk-taking by ordinary people as well as of companies.[2]

Health is no different when it comes to the issue of risk. Everyone runs the risk of getting sick, of course, and there's also the risk that someone may not recover if he or she gets sick.[3] In your role as a patient or potential patient, you tend to focus on keeping yourself healthy—that is, avoiding the risk of getting sick—and on how you're going to ensure treatment if you do get sick. Another kind of risk in the world of health involves whether the drugs you take are safe and effective. That's where federal involvement with prescription drugs began.

People without medical training typically know little about the effects of potent drugs and seldom know how much to take, at least not without some guidance. If the government didn't intervene to assure you that drugs are safe to swallow, there would be greater risks in taking them. (To be sure, the government regulators are sometimes criticized legitimately about dropping the ball, but overall prescription drugs are safe and effective when they make it to market.) The government today regulates both drug companies and how drugs are made available to their customers. Government programs encourage and regulate the activities of pharmaceutical companies as they discover, test, and manufacture drugs. The Food and Drug Administration (FDA) has the final say on which drugs can be sold and regulates whether you need to get a prescription for the most powerful medicines. A pharmacy that sells a prescription drug without a prescription is breaking the law—a law enforced so tightly that even alleged violations are rare. In all these ways, the government reduces your risk when you take your medicine.[4]

When it comes to how much those medicines cost, though, the government has largely had a hands-off policy. Yes, some intermittent attention to the issue has been paid. Almost 50 years ago, Senator Estes Kefauver held hearings to investigate why the first generation of new drugs cost so much. In 2003, Congress debated the cost of the new Medicare drug benefit. But the United States has never had a consistent policy on drug costs. The pharmaceutical companies have been left to charge what the market will bear for their products. That was fine as long as people only took prescription drugs occasionally, mostly for acute episodes of illness. Today, thanks to tremendous scientific advances, medicines are taken at a much greater rate; some medicines are taken every day for a lifetime.

Rising usage and growing prices fuel a widening discussion about how to solve a problem that more and more people recognize is at a crisis point. But the discussion seems to have reached an impasse. Doctors complain about the costs of drugs on behalf of their patients and so do patients themselves. The pharmaceutical industry responds that high drug prices are needed to finance the discovery of new medicines to benefit the patients. As the two

*Rising usage and growing prices fuel a widening discussion about how to solve a problem that more and more people recognize is at a crisis point. But the discussion seems to have reached an impasse.*

sides talk past each other, recommendations consistently focus only on changing the details of drug distribution.

It's time for a new debate on new terrain. In this book, we assess recent changes in the pharmaceutical industry in depth—not only the expanding scientific revolution, but also the business of pharmaceuticals. We look at the lack of progress that results from the blockbuster mentality. We explain how the drug industry operates, how new drugs are discovered, and how the government affects and controls these processes. These are the prerequisites to understanding how to lower drug prices.

Our examination shows that changes—built on the best aspects of today's pharmaceutical industry but fixing what's broken in our system—can reduce prices *and* improve the flow of new drugs that best serve society's needs. Sounds implausible? The pharmaceutical industry's mantra that high prices are the only way to ensure innovation has certainly permeated the psyche, but there really *is* an alternative. It requires bold, but achievable, action. We have a plan that *will* lower prices while ensuring access for all citizens to today's great medicines and tomorrow's new, revolutionary drug therapies.

## *Endnotes*

[1] Angell, Marcia. 2004. *The Truth about the Drug Companies: How They Deceive Us and What to Do about It.* New York: Random House. See also: Avorn, Jerry. 2004. *Powerful Medicines: The Benefits, Risks, and Costs of Prescription Drugs.* New York: Knopf. See also: Kassirer, Jerome P. 2005. *On the Take: How America's Complicity with Big Business Can Endanger Your Health.* New York: Oxford University Press.

[2] Moss, David. 2002. *When All Else Fails.* Cambridge, Mass.: Harvard University Press.

[3] Arrow, K. J. 1963. Uncertainty and the welfare economics of medical care. *American Economic Review* 53:5, 941–73.

[4] Temin, Peter. 1980. *Taking Your Medicine: Drug Regulation in the United States.* Cambridge, Mass.: Harvard University Press.

# CHAPTER ONE

## DRUGS AND DRUG PRICES

*If you want the rainbow, you gotta put up with the rain.*

—Dolly Parton

Is it any wonder that there's such a huge outcry about prescription drugs, particularly their high cost? Consider this: If your only source of information was commercial television, no one could fault you for thinking that GERD was a public health crisis in the United States on the scale of AIDS in Africa. In the time it takes you to read this paragraph, you can reasonably assume that American TV watchers saw dozens of advertisements encouraging them to check with their doctors to make sure they don't need to treat GERD with the Purple Pill.

What's GERD? It's the acronym for *gastrointestinal esophageal reflux disease*, commonly known as acid reflux disease—a condition in which the stomach releases an acid back into the esophagus. Until the 1980s, physicians rarely used the term, and when they did mention GERD it was probably to describe a complication of a rare pancreatic disorder. But that was before drugs like Zantac and Nexium came onto the market.[1]

In the late 1970s, drugs began to be introduced to reduce the acidity in the gastrointestinal tract, which is a source of unpleasant symptoms that can sometimes be related to serious illness. These innovative drugs worked so effectively that they were imitated and, by the end of the 1980s, at least four drugs were doing very well in the marketplace: Zantac, Tagamet, Pepcid, and Axid. Then, in the 1990s, the next generation of acid-reducing medicines, with more elegant molecular mechanisms, became even bigger blockbusters than the originals. You know them as Prilosec, Nexium, and Prevacid.

In 1981, Glaxo (now part of GlaxoSmithKline) introduced *Zantac*, the trade name for ranitidine, for the control of gastrointestinal acidity. This chemically innovative drug inhibits the stomach's production of acid, and its underlying process won its discoverer a Nobel Prize. While actually the second entrant in its therapeutic class (some call this a "me-too" drug), after *Tagamet* (cimetidine), Zantac had few adverse side effects and few negative interactions with other drugs. Glaxo wanted to match the success Smith, Kline, & French (also now part of GlaxoSmithKline) had with Tagamet and produced an excellent medicine—one promoted aggressively at a premium price.[2]

The initial indication for Zantac and similar drugs was to control and treat peptic ulcer disease. Manufacturers commissioned economic cost-benefit analyses to demonstrate that the drugs saved money by reducing the need for hospitalizations and surgical procedures, and the anti-ulcer drug market grew rapidly. But as successful as Zantac was in this market, a much larger market remained untapped—but not for long.

Physicians soon began to prescribe Zantac *off label*—in other words, for something other than what the drug was approved for (it's perfectly legal to do this)—to control symptoms of acid reflux from the stomach to the esophagus and throat. Glaxo saw an opportunity and quickly won approval from the U.S. Food and Drug Administration (FDA) for its drug to be prescribed to treat GERD. For some people, GERD can lead to serious illness if left untreated—but most people who take medicines such as Zantac are not part of that at-risk population.

Tens of millions of people now have a box of Zantac or Prilosec, which are no longer prescription drugs, in their medicine cabinets. You take them when you have *heartburn*—a condition experienced episodically or chronically by millions of people. What was once classified as simply a physical discomfort has been medicalized

> *While you're busy buying and taking those pills for something that you're now told is a "disease," a drug company is reaping the profits.*

by association with a sometimes serious disorder. And while you're busy buying and taking those pills for something that you're now told is a disease, a drug company is reaping the profits.[3]

The Zantac story illustrates how business has encroached on science in the world of pharmaceuticals. It's surely not the most monumental example: The drug's importance pales in comparison to cancer treatments, HIV drugs, or a number of others for much more serious diseases. But how Zantac came to be in your medicine cabinet is symptomatic of something that happens with drugs for more life-threatening conditions.

"There's little point in diagnosing a disease until something can be done to treat it," a physician colleague of ours is fond of saying. His point is aptly illustrated by the popularity of Zantac and several other new medication classes. As the focus of new drugs went from treating acute ailments such as infections to chronic ailments such as depression, drug companies set out to expand the markets for their products. When newly discovered drugs had beneficial effects that went beyond existing diseases they could treat, the industry worked to instill among consumers the idea that there was something very troubling these drugs *could* "cure." Some critics have called this *medicalizing* ordinary life.

There are plenty of other examples of medicalization. For instance, who hasn't been disgusted by seeing that nasty dermatophyte, Digger, in television advertisements for Lamisil? For as long as humans have been around, we've had to live with disfigurement, particularly of the toenails, caused by tiny fungal organisms. *Onycomycosis*, the technical name for toenail fungus, was never thought of as a disease. The condition is more of a cosmetic irritation than anything else, so you just endured it. Topical ointments and creams were of no use because the infection is internal to the nail surface. Nail fungus does respond to older, orally taken antifungal antibiotics, but these drugs came with some unpleasant side effects and large risks, particularly to the liver. So, doctors rarely offered any treatment for this condition.

Then came Lamisil, a new, "safer" antifungal drug approved by the FDA to treat onycomycosis. Annual sales of Lamisil exceed several hundred million dollars. People don't want Digger living in their toenails.

The drug Flomax is another example. It was approved by the FDA for treatment of *benign prostatic hyperplasia (BPH)*, a condition men face as they age. The prostate gland slowly enlarges, which may cause it to press on the urethra and cause a slower and less forceful flow of urine. The symptoms can be triggered by more serious diseases such as prostate cancer, a bladder infection, or bladder cancer, but having BPH is not a sign of risk for these conditions. It's more a part of the normal cycle of life. And while BPH can be a sign, in some instances, of more serious troubles, whose grandpa doesn't suffer the inconvenience of getting up in the middle of the night to visit the bathroom?

Boehringer Ingelheim's advertisements for Flomax are everywhere. The target audience isn't just BPH sufferers, but "people who care about men with symptoms." If men complain to their doctors that they are getting up in the middle of the night and their wives complain about being disturbed while sleeping, doctors are more likely to prescribe the drug to address what may well be a lifestyle or convenience issue. The financial stakes in encouraging the use of Flomax are huge: "The incidence of BPH is estimated to equal the age of the men. Therefore, 50 percent of men in their 50s have the disease, and this increases to 80 percent for those in their 80s."[4]

This example appears to be a case of the medicalization of something that is more an inconvenience for most patients than a real health problem. Oftentimes, it's the satirists who show you the truth. Flomax has been spoofed on *Saturday Night Live* through a parody advertisement for "Urigro" for the treatment of "weak male urination syndrome." The parody suggests you turn your weak stream (which the Flomax ads underline) into something a man can be proud of.

There's nothing wrong with medications for inconvenient urination or heartburn or athlete's foot. But if you want to understand why drugs cost so much in the United States, you can't avoid this discussion of medicalization. And the discussion is tied intimately to the "blockbuster" model that drives the pharmaceutical industry.

## The "Blockbuster" Mentality

Reports show that pharmaceutical companies spend hundreds of millions of dollars to develop a new drug, even in excess of $1 billion. A 2003 study by the Tufts Center for the Study of Drug Development estimated the cost at about $897 million, driven in large part by the pharmaceutical companies' search for thousands of molecules that *never* become drugs. This is a substantial increase from the estimated $500 million that the pharmaceutical industry spent in 1996, as reported by the Center. Drug firms say prices for new drugs are so high because they need to recover the investment in all those failed efforts and compensate for the risk of a promising new chemical entity that ultimately does not work as a drug. No wonder, then, that since the late 1970s pharmaceutical companies have focused so much of their attention on discovering market blockbusters.[5]

What makes a drug a blockbuster? In the pharmaceutical industry, a *blockbuster drug* is one that achieves acceptance by prescribing physicians as a therapeutic *standard* for, most commonly, a highly prevalent chronic (rather than *acute*) condition. Patients often take the medicines for long periods. And then there's the financial component of the definition. A blockbuster drug is typically defined as achieving annual worldwide sales exceeding $1 billion. Those staggering revenues are generated by two components: the large number of patients who take the medicine and the premium price typically charged (compared to the older drug it replaced). Long-term use by patients, often consistent with guidelines issued by professional physician organizations, creates an annuity for the pharmaceutical company—at least until the patent protection runs out.

Many individuals who follow the prescribed treatments realize benefits that include long-term control of symptoms and signs of illness, and improved qualify of life. But on the scientific side, a key point to make is that blockbuster drugs are, in essence, "one-size-fits-all" therapies. That fact alone feeds their market success.

Notably, fewer than 10 percent of new drugs introduced to the market achieve the blockbuster degree of success. But considering the potential financial results, the pharmaceutical companies keep trying to develop blockbusters.[6]

Since Zantac's introduction in 1981, many other new drugs have grown to blockbuster status, including medicines to treat high blood pressure and high cholesterol, depression and anxiety, and asthma and allergies—to name several of the most successful therapeutic classes. You'll surely recognize the names of a few of the 100 or so blockbuster drugs that have made it to market. Again, if you're a TV watcher, then you've likely heard about Ambien, Lipitor, Nexium, or Plavix, to name a few. Based just on how many times you've seen the commercials, you can imagine the revenues these drugs generate for the manufacturer.

Researchers know that large numbers of people benefit from taking prescribed blockbusters, but they also know from clinical trial results that some proportion of patients—sometimes quite large, depending on the drug—do *not* benefit. Often, when patients are taking multiple drugs and feeling better, no one can tell which drugs help and which don't; so, the patient continues with them all. And in still other cases, medicines are used inappropriately, in insufficient doses, or for too short a time for patients to benefit. From a profit point of view, though, it doesn't matter: In every case, the manufacturer still generates sales revenue.

> *Often, when patients are taking multiple drugs and feeling better, no one can tell which drugs help and which don't; so, the patient continues with them all.*

A class of drugs called *leukotriene modifiers*—you've probably heard of Singulair—is a good example of this phenomenon. These drugs offer significant benefits in controlling asthma symptoms, although many of the patients who tried them in clinical trials experienced no relief. Nevertheless, these medicines are popular with asthma sufferers partly because they can be taken orally on a daily basis, rather than having to fuss with a combination of other medications and unpopular inhalers. Plus, side effects are infrequent.[7]

It's impossible to know for sure who benefits from taking Singulair or similar medicines for asthma symptoms. If a patient takes the drug in combination with other medicines and enjoys symptomatic relief, how could you gauge the relative contributions of the individual drugs? Right now, there is *no* way. The point is that if a laboratory test or some other diagnostic method comes along for predicting which patients actually benefit, the market for this class of medicines will likely decline, as will sales revenue. Therefore, the "one-size-fits-all" blockbuster drug will always have a better financial profile. And those blockbusters are going to cost you—the consumer—serious money.

## Drugs for Smaller Patient Populations Drive Costs Even Higher

Annual sales of $1 billion are a strong incentive to focus on block-busters and the large patient populations to which they can be marketed. The flipside is a disincentive to develop drugs for smaller markets. In 1983, in an effort to mitigate the problem, Congress enacted *orphan drug legislation* that gives market exclusivity to firms that introduce medicines with U.S. target populations of less than 200,000 and establishes difficult hurdles for potential competitors seeking to prove superiority of a new drug.[8]

With the orphan drug law, you see the beginnings of a premium-pricing model for new, smaller-market therapies. In a sense, it's the opposite of the blockbuster model. When Genzyme Corporation developed Ceredase and Cerazyme to treat *Gaucher's disease*, a rare genetic disorder of lipid metabolism that afflicts (among others) Jews of Eastern European descent, the potential U.S. patients numbered only in the thousands. Without the new drug, patients would likely die in childhood. But Genzyme found an enzyme extracted from placentas (later synthesized using recombinant DNA techniques) to be fully curative of the disorder. The market protection for its orphan drug made it possible for Genzyme to turn a profit, selling very small quantities of the drug at a very high price. In 2002, the price for an annual course of treatment was approximately $170,000, but few insured patients with a prescription drug benefit had any difficulty accessing the medicine or getting reimbursement. That was because the number of people with Gaucher's disease is so small that the cost impact on insurers is minimal when averaged over all insured patients. Genzyme achieved early market success and substantial revenues.[9] Other biotech firms addressed small "niche" or "boutique" drug markets. Biogen developed one of the first efficacious treatments for *multiple sclerosis (MS)*, a neuromuscular degenerative disease of autoimmune origin that afflicts only around 400,000 people in the United States. (In the world of pharmaceuticals, you'll often hear about "efficacy" and "effectiveness." In this context, *efficacy* is the ability to produce a specifically desired effect, and is usually demonstrated in clinical trials. *Effectiveness* is demonstrated in practice.) Immunex developed a new treatment for rheumatoid arthritis (RA), a condition affecting only some 300,000 U.S. patients.[10] Like Genzyme's new drug, these drugs need to be taken every day for the rest of a patient's life, or until something better comes along—at a substantial cost.[11]

These examples set the new *premium-pricing model* for new, smaller-market drug therapies. It was a model that fit for many drug introductions that followed, including for *Crohn's disease*, a progressive gastrointestinal disorder of autoimmune origin; allergies and asthma; psoriasis; fungus infections afflicting immunocompromised patients; and the new, targeted cancer therapies. The model applied even to a stalwart class of drugs: antibacterial antibiotics. There's always a need for new antibiotic medications because the evolution of disease-causing organisms leads to drug resistance. New antibiotics are typically reserved by doctors for patients who aren't responding to any of the older drugs, and so the market size and revenues are limited. But these antibiotic drugs are sold at a premium pricing level, which is exactly how the few totally new antibiotics introduced in the past two decades have entered the market. The model also applies to the major advances achieved in the treatment of HIV/AIDS, which were once nearly always fatal but are now treatable, chronic conditions. The high prices, though, limit access in the developing world, where HIV/AIDS is far more prevalent.

The latest wave of scientific advances, which facilitates new approaches to select therapies for ill patients, promises to raise even greater cost challenges. The sequencing of the human genome gives scientists detailed information about the functions of a number of genes, and drugs are being developed to correct, ameliorate, or otherwise address genetic defects that lead to disease. And in theory, it's even possible to test—with high confidence—which patients with a given defect will benefit from the treatment.

*How much higher will drug prices go with these new therapies?*

How much higher will drug prices go with these new therapies? They come at a very high cost, according to a *Business Week* article reviewing new cancer therapies, titled "Going Broke to Stay Alive." Among other drugs, the story discusses Gleevec, a Novartis drug that treats two forms of cancer associated with a single genetic defect, and Genentech's Herceptin, which treats a hereditary form of breast cancer that afflicts some 15–25 percent of all patients who develop the disease. Gleevec specifically targets a genetic defect and is highly efficacious in the target group of cancer patients and responsible for significant increases in patient survival, but does nothing for patients with other forms of cancer who do not have the genetic defect. Herceptin has an antibody that targets only patients whose genomes include the BRCA-1 gene; in other words, it interferes with the progression of the cancer. A diagnostic test predicts with high confidence which patients are candidates for the therapy. This drug also increases a patient's chances for survival compared to earlier therapeutic approaches.[12]

Gleevec costs $2,200 a month and can be taken indefinitely, while Herceptin runs $3,200 a month, with an additional expense of $100 a pill for an anti-nausea drug to relieve side effects. Hence the article's title. Gleevec's annual revenues were $2.2 billion, exceeding the blockbuster threshold, while Herceptin's revenues were near $1 billion a year between 1998 and 2005.[13]

Targeted therapies aimed at a specific patient's unique characteristics will only become more common. But the costs to patients and payers (insurance companies and health plans) are becoming more and more prohibitive. Even the director of the National Institutes of Health acknowledges that the overall cost society pays for drugs cannot be reduced unless people stop taking drugs from which they don't realize much (or any) benefit.

How will the marketplace for pharmaceuticals respond to monumental scientific breakthroughs and the new model for premium pricing for smaller target populations?[14] To what degree do we have to fail to capitalize on scientific and technological advances before policy makers have had enough? Which therapies that *might* work, but never get developed, have to fall by the wayside before people demand that our broken system be fixed? Are you willing to watch your loved ones suffer while business considerations get in the way of taking the next steps to get needed medicines?

If prices keep rising, many more people will lose access to needed medicines. If the drug companies don't take in billions in profits, they claim they'll have to put the brakes on innovation. The incentives are all askew and society's interests get short shrift in the fallout. Business decisions encroach on medical advances—a situation *none* of us can afford.

To understand just how big a deal this is, let's explore one scientific breakthrough that is suffering from this condition.

## *Business Decisions Encroach on Medical Advances*

Scientific and technological advances make it possible for researchers to focus on the differences in how individuals respond to medicines by identifying sequences of human genes that correlate with whether patients will benefit from a given treatment. This concept is a veritable revolution in clinical drug development—the long-anticipated *personalized medicine*. This revolution is driven by something called *biomarkers*, which are fragments of DNA sequences that cause disease or are associated with susceptibility to disease.

So far, disease-specific or drug-specific biomarkers have been identified for chronic diseases, including diabetes and asthma, as well as various forms of cancer. Herceptin, which was discussed previously, is possibly the best example of a current drug whose use depends on the presence of a genomic biomarker. There's even a molecular diagnostic test to predict which breast cancer patients will benefit from treatment. This is only the beginning. As scientists pore through huge volumes of data collected from sequencing the full human genome (people's genetic makeup) and relate the data to observations in the laboratory and to presentations of disease symptoms, they're going to discover many, many more biomarkers.

We don't use the word *revolution* lightly. Biomarkers already have a great influence over how clinical trials are designed and conducted. If researchers can develop a molecular diagnostic test, based on their knowledge of biomarkers, to predict which patients will benefit from taking a medicine, clinical trials can enroll a more homogeneous group and conceivably fewer human subjects and still be able to establish whether a new drug is superior to an earlier therapeutic alternative. It's the kind of cutting-edge scientific advance pharmaceutical firms should fully embrace.

But what if we told you that this tremendous medical breakthrough is being squandered in the name of profit or out of competitive fear? What if we told you that patients are not accessing potentially powerful cancer medications as fully as possible because of a *business* issue with biomarkers?

Scientists working in large pharmaceutical firms tell us that *financial* considerations are getting in the way of fully and rapidly realizing the promise of biomarkers. Who loses? All of us. Consider the tale of Iressa and Tarceva.

In the 1960s, scientists observed that kinase enzymes play an essential role in the growth of certain cancers, and so they began to explore how to block the action of kinase. It took decades before the first kinase inhibitor drug made it to market. In 2001, Novartis introduced Gleevec, "hailed as a miracle drug poised to usher in a new age in cancer treatment."[15] The drug targets genetic aberrations leading to two infrequently occurring cancers, chronic myeloid leukemia and gastrointestinal stromal tumors.[16] As we previously mentioned, therapy with this drug has produced major survival benefits for patients.

Iressa and Tarceva are two newer targeted kinase inhibitors, which address genetic mutations that have major roles in producing certain types of *non-small cell lung cancer (NSCLC)*, a condition for which older chemotherapies have not produced much survival benefit. (These drugs are also used on or off label to treat a number of other cancers.) Iressa, approved—although with some controversy—by the FDA in 2003, was discovered and developed by AstraZeneca. While only about 10 percent of patients in the trials for Iressa demonstrated shrinkage in tumor size, the FDA gave its okay to get this much-needed therapy to market quicker.

Once the drug was on the market, published reports showed that patients appeared to develop serious complications disproportionately, including lung disease and stroke.[17] Late in 2004 and early in 2005, two clinical trials demonstrated convincingly that patients treated with Iressa did not live longer than those treated with traditional chemotherapy. Meanwhile, many oncologists were observing striking improvements—including arrested disease progression and extended survival—among a small proportion of NSCLC patients they were treating. Several academic and commercial research groups, all independent of AstraZeneca, went on to develop laboratory tests that appear to predict which small, specific subgroups of patients with NSCLC actually benefit from this drug. It appeared that a biomarker was at work here, so the FDA reviewed the new information and, late in 2005, required a change in Iressa's label. The FDA severely restricted access to the drug to those most likely to benefit.[18] AstraZeneca could no longer reap the profits through sales of the drug to people for whom it wasn't likely to work.

The FDA's reclassification of Iressa was made easier because of the agency's experience with Tarceva, a drug that competes with Iressa. Tarceva was discovered by a small research firm, then developed by a larger biotechnology company, and today is distributed by the pharmaceutical firm that now owns a majority stake in the developer. Clinical trials were outsourced. Using biomarkers, Tarceva's human studies demonstrate an improved survival of additional months, among NSCLC patients who continue to be treated with it, compared to patients receiving traditional chemotherapy.

The point here is that Iressa's manufacturers did not bother to identify a biomarker predictive of the drug's response or toxicity—at least not for the FDA. In fact, the pharmaceutical industry has been quite slow to embrace, at least publicly, the concept of biomarker-enabled medications. Iressa's biomarker was identified by the university researchers in Boston and New York, and only after they observed that the drug produced unmistakable benefits in an extremely small proportion of patients.

## Sacrificed on the Altar of "Market Size"

The extent to which the large R & D-based pharmaceutical firms have developed, or are developing, capabilities to use biomarkers in drug development is somewhat of a mystery. Why? Most likely, they fear that if they predict which specific patients will benefit from a new drug, it will reduce the size of its potential market. After all, as explained above, when a drug is approved for use in all patients— rather than just the few who are predicted to benefit—the drug maker earns revenue even from patients that the medicine *doesn't* help.

One startup in the Boston-area cluster of biopharmaceutical firms attracted investors to its business model of partnering with big pharmaceutical firms to search for genomic biomarkers that were specific to drugs in development, particularly targeting common chronic diseases. But there was little interest in such partnerships among pharmaceutical firms. The insurance carriers, though, saw the financial advantage if expensive drugs were given *only* to those patients with a high likelihood of benefiting. Those carriers pay for medicines.

In 2005, the FDA issued what it calls a "guidance" on the use of genomic data and biomarkers in drug development, aimed at encouraging firms to engage in such work at least on an exploratory basis.[19] The FDA's initiative offers pharmaceutical firms that collect data on genomic biomarkers a "safe harbor" to submit confidentially what its researchers use "internally," so the FDA can use this information to gain a better understanding of the potential for improving the effectiveness and efficiency of drug development. The FDA promises these pharmaceutical firms that the data won't be used to limit approval for a new medicine only for use in patients who can be identified from biomarkers. However, the drug firms, securely tied to their blockbuster mentality, remain unconvinced.

Not long ago, Pfizer was forced to suspend its clinical trials for a new cholesterol-lowering drug because the researchers were finding high levels of toxicity. It was a tremendous disappointment for the company, which had hoped to combine the new drug with its blockbuster, Lipitor, and thus extend the patent life—and also the blockbuster status—of its cash cow. If biomarkers were part of the picture, might things have turned out differently? No one can say for sure. But it's reasonable to assume that if Pfizer had opted for a strategy to identify a biomarker for the percentage of patients who wouldn't have the toxicity found in the large trial population, then the outcome would probably have been a viable drug. Yes, it would have a much smaller market. No, it would not rake in the cash like a blockbuster. But patients would benefit. Now, there is no new drug. (More on this story in Chapter 7, "How to Lower Drug Prices.")

Without proper and sensible incentives, it's no wonder the pharmaceutical firms all too often think like businesspeople concerned only about their shareholders rather than like scientists who work for the good of society. Can Americans afford such an impasse? Should we let business concerns determine whether new, innovative medicines get into the hands of prescribing doctors and their patients who need treatment? Wouldn't society's interests be best served by moving forward aggressively to realize the full scientific value of biomarkers?

*Should we let business concerns determine whether new, innovative medicines get into the hands of prescribing doctors and their patients who need treatment?*

Consider another example. A group of students in an MIT class taught by one of the authors built a model of personalized medicine for asthma, using a medicine mentioned earlier—Merck's drug Singulair. They found plenty of available scientific knowledge that would make it relatively easy to develop a genetic test to identify which patients would respond positively to Singulair for their asthma. Today, Singulair is a blockbuster, but it must be the case that tens of thousands of patients who buy it realize little or no benefit. The students estimated that limiting the drug's use only to those who "passed" such a test would increase the efficacy rate of Singulair by a huge margin. But it would also reduce Merck's revenues by more than a third.

Everyone who takes Singulair but doesn't fully benefit enriches Merck and depletes society's resources available for medical treatment. But where are the incentives for the pharmaceutical companies to do business in any other way?

The complexity of the U.S. marketplace has increased since 1980 as the portion of health costs consumed by medicines has nearly doubled. Many private insurers and managed care plans that offer a drug benefit have made it difficult for doctors to prescribe costly, brand-name medicines. Often, that restricts a patient's access to innovative therapies. For blockbuster drugs with large target populations, payers frequently engage the services of so-called *pharmaceutical benefits management (PBM)* firms (more about these in Chapter 3, "The Drug Industry Today") These third-party organizations negotiate discounts from drug manufacturers on behalf of the payers in exchange for helping "move market share" to one drug and away from the competition. For the premium-priced orphan drugs, many payers establish strict criteria for patient selection, restricting access to a small proportion of its covered population. This keeps the impact of their high costs relatively low when spread over a large insured population. The industry calls this measure *costs per member, per month*. But as more of these targeted therapies enter the market, concerns about the cost impact only heighten.[20]

Payers also face costs for diagnostic tests required for some of the newest, most innovative targeted therapies. These tests, which come at a significant cost, predict a prospective patient's response to treatment. Payers have to figure out a cost-effective process that facilitates access to the most expensive drugs for those who will benefit from them. It's uncharted territory.

The situation seems to go from bad to worse. Scientific advances only spur higher drug prices. Does it have to be this way? Why has the problem gotten so out of hand?

## *How We Got Here*

The proportion of healthcare dollars expended on prescription pharmaceuticals in the United States has risen dramatically in recent years, and today, prescription drugs are a critical part of our healthcare and our lives. Demand for medicines is high because they genuinely contribute significantly to our health, our well-being, and the quality of our lives. But the improvements are so often overshadowed by how much money we have to spend to get those treatments. It's especially bad for the elderly. Why do senior citizens have to spend nearly $2,000 per month, on average, on their medicines? Why should senior citizens have to travel to another country to save money when they buy their medicines?

The pharmaceutical industry has a stock answer to the cost question. Drug companies contend that research costs hundreds of millions of dollars that they have to recover. They note that they're continuing to do the research that cures diseases and saves lives. And because they take all the financial risks associated with discovering new drugs, then they cannot lower drug prices without reducing the flow of new drugs. (One company's current drug ads end with the phrase "today's medicines finance tomorrow's miracles.")

Surely no one would argue against maintaining the stream of innovative new products that emerge from research. So, what's the solution?

We have an answer. To understand *why* our solution makes sense, though, you need to understand how today's medicines were discovered, approved, and introduced to the market. Why does this history matter? Because it's crucial to see that although the process by which drugs make it to the market is undergoing a radical change, the ways in which their prices are ultimately determined remains mired in the old world.

An innovative approach is needed, a better way to make sure new and better drugs can continue to flow to consumers at a reasonable cost. Our solution makes sense when you grasp the nature of the changes. So, we're going to look more closely at drug discovery and development, and explore the transformation of the pharmaceutical industry's structure. Building on this examination, we offer a solution that will lower drug prices without interrupting the flow of new drugs. It's a solution that fits this new world.

# *Endnotes*

[1] Harrison, Tinsley Randolph. 1977. *Harrison's Principles of Internal Medicine.* 8th ed. New York: McGraw-Hill.

[2] Wright, R. 1996. How Zantac became the best-selling drug in history. *Journal of Health Care Marketing* 16(4): 24–29.

[3] Barsky, A. 1995. Somatization and medicalization in the era of managed care. *JAMA* 274(24): 1931–34.

[4] Johns Hopkins Medical Institutions. Severe form of "enlarged prostate" disease discovered. Newswise. www.newswise.com/articles/view/527121/?sc=rsmn (accessed April 18, 2007).

[5] Tufts Center for the Study of Drug Development. 2003. Total cost to develop a new prescription drug, including cost of post-approval research, is $897 million. http://155.212.10.127/NewsEvents/RecentNews.asp?newsid=29 (accessed April 18, 2007).

[6] Grabowski, H. and J. Vernon. 1994. Returns to R & D on new drug introductions in the 1980s. *Journal of Health Economics* 13(4): 383–406. See also: Lynn, Mathew. 1992. The Billion Dollar Battle: Merck Vs. Glaxo. London: Trafalgar Square Publishing.

[7] Sorkness, C. A. 2001. Leukotriene receptor antagonists in the treatment of asthma. *Pharmacotherapy* March 21 (3Pt2): 34S–37S.

[8] Rohde, D. 2000. The Orphan Drug Act: An engine of innovation? at what cost? *Food and Drug Law Journal* 55(1): 125–43.

[9] Elias, P. 2003. "Orphan drugs save lives, but who pays?" Associated Press. May 23.

[10] National Multiple Sclerosis Society. About MS. www.nationalmssociety.org/site/PageServer?pagename=HOM_ABOUT_homepage (accessed April 18, 2007).

[11] Thomson CenterWatch. Drugs approved by the FDA: Drug name—Enbrel (etanercept). www.centerwatch.com/patient/drugs/dru737.html (accessed April 18, 2007).

[12] Arnst, C. 2006. Going broke to stay alive. *Business Week* January 30. See also: National Cancer Institute. 2001. Imatinib mesylate (Gleevec). www.cancer.gov/clinicaltrials/digestpage/gleevec (accessed April 18, 2007). See also: American Cancer Society. 2005. Herceptin "revolutionary" for breast cancer. October 20. www.cancer.org/docroot/NWS/content/NWS_1_1x_Breast_ Cancer_Studies_Show_Survival_Benefit_When_Herceptin_Used_Early.asp (accessed April 18, 2007). See also: O'Brien, S. et al. 2003. Imatinib compared with interferon and low-dose cytarabine for newly diagnosed chronic-phase chronic myeloid leukemia. *New England Journal of Medicine* 348(11): 994–1004.

[13] Langreth, R. and M. Herper. 2006. Pill pushers: How the drug industry abandoned science for salesmanship. *Forbes* May 8. www.forbes.com/free_forbes/2006/0508/

094a.html (accessed April 18, 2007). See also: Roche Investor Update. 2005. Twice as many long-term survivors with HER2-positive metastatic breast cancer following treatment with Herceptin. Roche. May 17. www.roche.com/inv-update-2005-05-17b (accessed April 18, 2007). See also: Winslow, R. 2006. Betting on a new cancer drug. *Wall Street Journal,* June 15:B1.

[14] Zerhouni, E. A. 2006. Personalized medicine. Presentation April 18 at the 3rd Annual World Health Care Congress, Washington, D.C.

[15] Boyles, S. 2006. Five years later, Gleevec fights cancer: Study shows high survival rate for patients with chronic myeloid leukemia. *WebMD Medical News* Dec. 6. www.medicinenet.com/script/main/art.asp?articlekey=77983 (accessed April 18, 2007).

[16] O'Brien et al., *op. cit.* See also: National Cancer Institute, *op. cit.*

[17] U.S. Food and Drug Administration. 2005. FDA consumer magazine updates: clinical trial of Iressa. March-April. www.fda.gov/fdac/departs/2005/205_upd.html#iressa (accessed April 18, 2007). See also: Reuters Health Information. 2002. Japan links 81 deaths to cancer drug Iressa. Dec. 5. www.cancerpage.com/news/article.asp?id=5244 (accessed April 18, 2007).

[18] Medical News Today. 2005. US label change for cancer drug Iressa (gefitinib). June 18. www.medicalnewstoday.com/medicalnews.php?newsid=26352 (accessed April 18, 2007).

[19] U.S. Food and Drug Administration. 2005. FDA issues final Guidance on pharmacogenomic submissions. *FDA News, Drug Daily Bulletin* 2(62): March 29.

[20] Pharmaceutical Care Management Association. 2005. *How Pharmacy Benefit Managers Help Employers Provide Safer, More Affordable Prescription Drug Benefits.* Washington, D.C.: PCMA. www.pcmanet.org/research/index.htm (accessed April 18, 2007).

# CHAPTER TWO

*The real voyage of discovery consists not in seeking new
landscapes but in having new eyes.*

—Marcel Proust

Over the past couple of generations, drugs have gone from being
occasionally beneficial to an indispensable component of medical
treatment. They treat acute infections and chronic conditions successfully. They address many disorders long recognized and others
undiagnosed until a short time ago. Some of today's market-leading
medications mitigate the risks of developing serious illnesses, reduce
the symptoms of others, and for many people lessen the impact of
disease on their daily lives.

Drugs weren't always as good as they are today. While doctors
have been "prescribing" drugs for centuries, proven efficacious medicines became available only during the latter half of the twentieth
century. (In the world of pharmaceuticals, you'll often hear about
"efficacy" and "effectiveness." In this context, *efficacy* is the ability to
produce a specifically desired effect, and is usually demonstrated in
clinical trials. *Effectiveness* is demonstrated in practice.)

Throughout most of the nineteenth century, drugs offered little
relief for patients. Noted physician and scholar Oliver Wendell
Holmes, Sr. of Harvard Medical School (father of the famous
Supreme Court justice) famously remarked in 1842, "If all the

medicines in the world were thrown into the sea, it would be all the better for mankind and all the worse for the fishes." By the late 1920s, only a handful of basic medicines had found their way into common medical practice: aspirin, codeine, and morphine for pain; digitalis, nitroglycerin, and quinine for heart disorders; and insulin for diabetes. These drugs offered the hope of controlling, but not curing, diseases. A few biological vaccines or antitoxins and only a couple of synthetic drugs were available for some infectious illnesses.[1]

Antibiotics, the earliest "wonder" drugs, were introduced in the 1930s. Extensive screening of chemical compounds began to find substances that were curative and would destroy disease-causing organisms without attacking the host. First came the sulfa drugs, then the penicillins, followed by the tetracyclines and others. These medicines formed the basis of the *armamentarium*—the complete range of equipment, medications, and techniques a medical practitioner has at his or her disposal—used to treat infections on World War II battlefields.[2] The "therapeutic revolution" was under way, with drugs increasingly at the center of medical practice.

Antibiotics truly are wonder drugs. They can *cure* disease—something few previously available medicines could do. Plus, you can actually measure and quantify the ability of an antibiotic to kill the bacteria that cause an illness, which means the efficacy of these drugs can be documented. The availability of the earliest antibiotics helped facilitate better understanding of how microorganisms caused disease. Once scientists could see clearly that existing medicines failed to target and destroy certain bacteria, they could search for new drugs to attack other parts of the spectrum of disease-producing bacteria. Scientists followed the same procedure as they observed that bacteria, over time, evolve to develop "resistance" to existing antibiotics.

By the 1950s, death rates due to bacterial infections and the duration of episodes of illness had both fallen precipitously, thanks to the availability of new medicines and the implementation of a number of public health initiatives. Some experts even brashly speculated that continued development of new antibiotics would eventually be a low priority. U.S. Surgeon General William Stewart, for example, told Congress in the late 1960s that the "time has come to close the book on infectious diseases. We have basically wiped out infection in the United States."[3]

Antibiotics were not the only big news on the medication front. With the 1950s came *corticosteroids* to treat inflammation, *rauwolfia alkaloids* that were active as tranquilizers and later antihypertensives, *antihistamines* to control nasal allergies, *xanthines* to alleviate the symptoms of asthma, and lots of other new drugs. Sometimes, doctors would find new uses for existing medicines when they noticed that a drug used to treat a particular condition had other beneficial, if unintended, effects. For example, *sulfa drugs* originally developed to treat infection were modified to control urine output as a way to treat high blood pressure.

For all the good they did, these "first-generation" drugs had some downsides. It was inconvenient to take an antacid *every hour* to relieve the symptoms of your peptic ulcer. Adverse side effects were much more troublesome. If you took medicine to control asthma symptoms, then your heart would beat faster. Antihistamines caused drowsiness. If you were lucky, the worst side effect of your antidepressant medication was dry mouth. Some interacted with certain foods and beverages to raise your blood pressure to a potentially fatal level. To put it kindly, many patients found that taking drugs was less than desirable, and more than a few would choose suffering the symptoms of debilitating illnesses over enduring the side effects of medicines their doctors prescribed. Yet, the march of pharmaceutical progress continued unabated.

By the 1960s, there were drugs in many of the therapeutic classes that are still doing much medical good today. Great advances in chemistry and the life sciences improved our understanding of how diseases work, particularly some for which we didn't yet have

of safety and efficacy before approving it for market. Some drugs were exempt—such as aspirin, which had been on the market prior to 1938—but all drugs introduced between 1938 and 1962 would undergo an expert review to determine whether they possessed substantial evidence of effectiveness. Most of the 4,000 drugs thus reviewed were deemed "possibly effective" or, at best, "probably effective."

After the 1962 law was enacted, an extensive debate unfolded over standards for approving new drugs. Eventually, the FDA opted for requiring well-designed clinical trials—a standard that continues today. Later, legislation in 1976 extended the FDA's authority to regulate "medical devices," also requiring evidence of safety and efficacy. Then, in 1984, some provisions of the *Hatch-Waxman Act* provided for more rapid availability of generic drugs after patent protection had expired, requiring no clinical trials but only that the applicant firm establish the generic's chemical and biological equivalence to the original drug.[7]

During this period of expanding regulation, with extensive government involvement in the pharmaceutical industry's business, the "therapeutic revolution" unfolded as described earlier. Today, physicians have at their disposal thousands of approved pharmaceuticals for a host of acute and chronic illnesses. For some disorders, doctors can even choose from several alternative drugs, and a number of medications introduced over the past 25 years offer the first effective drug therapy for previously unmet medical needs. The advances, though, aren't all breakthroughs at that level. Most of today's widely prescribed medications are actually new generations of more "user-friendly" drugs that replace earlier ones. Typically, these drugs have far fewer or much less bothersome side effects or can be taken less often, which means patients are more likely to take them as prescribed.

How do the drug companies decide which drugs to mass-produce and distribute, given all the scientific advances and the regulatory hurdles they have to scale to get a drug to market? The answer brings us back to potential revenue and the blockbuster model, and is key to understanding why we're in such a dire price situation today.

## Produce the Drugs That Make Big Money

In a Harvard Medical School classroom in the early 1970s, as the Vietnam War was winding down, a leading endocrinologist told his young, idealistic students in a lecture that *potassium permanganate*, a substance used widely in the chemistry lab, makes an excellent treatment for *goiter*, a benign thyroid condition. "You can borrow it from one of your colleagues in a research laboratory," he said. Students were puzzled. Why wasn't this effective treatment available as a prescription drug?

The professor explained that pharmaceutical firms don't invest the large sums of money needed to conduct clinical tests on a drug if it cannot be expected to generate a large amount of revenue. A small target population of patients with a particular disease makes it unattractive for the drug firms to address an unmet medical need. In some cases, a large enough *number* of patients might warrant moving forward, but they're primarily in the developing world—which usually means they'll have insufficient funds to purchase the drug. So, the drug companies balk. "These companies have a fiduciary responsibility to maximize monetary returns to their shareholders," the professor noted, "so they simply cannot develop such drugs."

The equation is much the same today. The promise of large numbers of patients to take new medicines, resulting in big sales revenues, drove (and still drives) most decisions by drug companies to invest in developing new drug candidates. But it's not the only way firms could produce large revenues. The pharmaceutical companies found that customers would tolerate very high prices to access medicines.

Then there's *off-label prescribing*—like what happened with Zantac. The FDA determines when and how a drug manufacturer can market a medicine, but doesn't regulate when and how doctors can prescribe that medicine. Prescribing a medication for something other than the "official" use for which the FDA gave approval is absolutely legal. Sometimes, off-label prescribing is supported by good scientific evidence; clinical research shows, or doctors find that medicines are effective in contexts other than those addressed during commercial drug development. Other times, it is encouraged by distorted information provided during the course of drug promotion. One example: *cerebral and peripheral vasodilators*, widely advertised by drug companies in the early 1980s for treatment of senile dementia, promoted the misinformation that the condition is caused by inadequate flow of blood to the brain.[8]

To be sure, off-label uses of drugs can provide important pathways to innovation in clinical practice, but when new uses are not formally studied—and most never are—the actual value the medicines bring to the treatment of disease will never be known. But why quibble with that sticky scientific issue? One study reported that more than 20 percent of drugs prescribed in the United States during 2001 were for uses inconsistent with the FDA approvals—and thus may have no real therapeutic value to those who take them. That translates to an estimated 150 million prescriptions and billions of dollars of additional sales.[9]

Are you outraged? Oddly, public outrage over the high costs of prescription medicines is a

*One study reported that more than 20 percent of drugs prescribed in the United States during 2001 were for uses inconsistent with the FDA approvals—and thus may have no real therapeutic value to those who take them.*

relatively recent phenomenon—despite the fact that drug prices in the United States have long been higher than those for other goods and services. Studies from the 1930s to the 1970s, when insurance coverage for medicines was essentially non-existent and you had to pay for your medicine out of pocket, concluded that doctors and patients alike neither knew much, nor were particularly concerned, about the prices of prescription drugs. In 1964, when federal law provided for the first government-funded health insurance for senior citizens, drug coverage wasn't even included.[10]

What changed? It has to do with treating *chronic* illnesses. The most widely prescribed medicines in the 1960s and 1970s addressed *acute* medical conditions—bacterial infections needing antibiotics and episodes of other disorders including allergies, asthma, anxiety, depression, or psychosis. It was some years later that so many drugs became widely available for the long-term treatment of persistent conditions. When patients might need to take a drug every day for the rest of their lives, they—and their insurers—start paying attention to the cost.

Beginning in the 1970s, stimulated in part by the growth of health insurance coverage, overall demand for healthcare in the United States began to increase—and still does. Drugs kept pace: As more drugs and different drugs entered the market, demand grew, following the overall trend. The new drugs introduced to supersede existing ones always came with higher prices. The pharmaceutical companies became more competitive, but not on price—*high* was a constant. They vied for market share on the basis of their new drugs' attributes.[11]

It became apparent, as the overall demand for healthcare rose and brought with it new cost concerns, that drugs were an aspect of healthcare where costs could be controlled. This was part of the rationale behind allowing for generic substitutes when drug patents expired. Making lower-priced generic medicines available was one way to control costs. By the 1970s, nearly every state had a law encouraging or requiring the substitution of generics for higher-cost brand-name drugs.

How did the drug companies respond? Remember, they want *revenue,* and generics take that away. So, they introduced new products. Some were "knockoffs," but many others were innovative. Drug development focused, more and more, on treatments for chronic conditions—that's where the big money could be made. Scientific breakthroughs encouraged the introduction of new approaches to therapy; many new drug entrants were, in effect, safer and more efficacious upgrades of members of already available drug classes. When the new drugs debuted at higher prices, and questions were raised, the pharmaceutical industry repeated the same mantra: These new drugs are better, higher quality, and offer more benefits.

A body of academic research by several generations of economists offered a way to think about the value of newer, higher-priced, higher-quality medicines. The origins of the approach date back to the 1920s, when economist Frederick Waugh observed certain attributes of asparagus for sale in Boston's Haymarket that he associated with higher quality. He noticed that the "best" asparagus, leafy and green, sold for higher prices than stalks that were either leafy *or* green but not both. He proposed a method to "value" the changes in prices of goods by relating it to the evolution of and improvement in their attributes.[12]

Waugh's method was refined over the years and has been applied to changes in the prices and values of residential real estate, automobiles, and computers, as well as prescription drugs. Based on published studies, we wouldn't be surprised to find that, in recent years, quality-adjusted drug prices continued to increase while those for computers and automobiles declined in some years by double digits.[13]

Whether you accept the drug companies' argument that "quality" warrants the prices we pay for their products in the United States, the reasons the high prices are of such concern are straightforward enough: They offer great benefits, and hence demand is great, but so many people can't afford them. How, then, do we make sure the people who need these medicines can get them at an affordable price? And how can we accomplish that objective while ensuring that adequate resources continue to be available for drug development, so that the stream of innovative medicines emerging from R & D continues? After all, the industry argues that forcing the prices lower will choke innovation. What is the link between prices and innovation?

## The Link between Drug Prices and Innovation

We can state it unequivocally: When it comes to pharmaceutical innovation, the United States knows no equal.

Following World War II, the United States and the rest of the industrialized world, particularly the countries of Europe, made very different choices about where to focus their policies and resources when it came to health. The Europeans focused on establishing national systems of healthcare delivery or financing. Meanwhile, the U.S. government—urged on by influential citizens and prominent scientists—chose to invest in a biomedical research infrastructure.

The results of that decision are in. After six decades, the National Institutes of Health (NIH), with its annual budget in excess of $28 billion, is unequalled in the scientific accomplishments it has stimulated and supported. NIH enjoys tremendous prestige and high public support well beyond the scientific community. The vast majority of the world's influential scientific journals are published in the United States. The influence of key scientific organizations, such as the National Academy of Sciences (NAS), extends well beyond our borders.

Scientific prestige is only part of the story. The economic development spawned by the U.S. biomedical research establishment is the envy of the world. While we've enjoyed the fruits of these investments, other countries have been very slow to follow. It has brought lots of jobs, but also high drug prices. In fact, drugs today cost more to consumers in the United States than almost anywhere else in the world.

The federal government does little to influence drug prices, essentially leaving the large healthcare payers and the large pharmaceutical firms to duke it out. In fact, strengthening this particular way of letting the market determine drug prices is a cornerstone of *Medicare Part D*, the new prescription drug benefit introduced in 2006 (and the subject of Chapter 5, "How *Not* to Lower Drug Prices"). But other national governments have adopted various kinds of price-control policies that keep their drug prices low. Many countries have national *formularies*, which list the drugs that are reimbursable by the national healthcare financing systems. Most other countries also set the rates at which medicines are sold or reimbursed. When new drugs are introduced to market in Germany, for example, the prices are typically set *in reference to*—meaning a small increment above the lower-priced, off-patent, generic drug it is replacing. One result of this scheme is that healthcare dollars in Germany go almost equally to wholesalers and pharmacists as they do to drug companies, which in turn limits the funds available for innovative research and development. And the program is alleged by its critics to limit patient access to drugs they need, compromising their chances of recovery.[14]

Some of these countries extend their regulations further to include limits on the amount of money a pharmaceutical company can spend to promote a drug. That's part of how the French government influences prices of and expenditures on drugs. And if a company breaches the advertising regulations, the government may actually cut the price of a drug. A few countries even supplement these "supplier side" controls with sanctions on doctors who prescribe "inappropriately," aiming to reduce the demand for medicines. In Germany, for instance, doctors who "over-prescribe" may be fined.

Of course, the situation isn't uniform. For example, drug prices are relatively high in the United Kingdom and much lower in France. The British government, which adopted fewer economic controls on medicines, regulates company profits but allows prices to be determined in the marketplace. The French government has stringent supplier-side controls.

While the United States is busy *not* regulating drug prices, U.S.-based companies or multinationals with U.S. research facilities are also busy innovating. A disproportionate share of innovative drugs, especially over the past 20 years, has been developed in the United States by these firms. That drug prices here are the highest in the world is directly related to this fact, very likely by cause and effect. It follows that a disproportionate share of drug profits accrues on U.S. sales.

In the year 2000, eight U.S.-based pharmaceutical firms were among the top 15 firms in terms of worldwide sales. That same year, 29 of 75 top-selling medicines globally originated in firms with corporate headquarters in the United States. Japan, the world's second-largest pharmaceutical market, did not have a single company among the top-selling 15 firms, and drug companies based there introduced only eight of the leading medicines. The United Kingdom, with the fewest economic controls on pharmaceuticals in Europe, accounted for 10 of the 75 top-selling medicines, while French firms introduced only three. The picture was the same for nearly every year during the 1990s.

To be sure, attributing a pharmaceutical firm's "nationality" to the location of its corporate headquarters is somewhat misleading in the globalized economy. GlaxoSmithKline, the world's second-largest drug maker in terms of sales, has its corporate headquarters in England but also has large-scale U.S. operations, particularly in research and development. The company employs about the same number of people in the United States as in the United Kingdom. The large Swiss company Novartis has its worldwide R & D headquarters in Massachusetts. And all of the large pharmaceutical firms are truly multinational, with drug development, manufacturing, and sales operations distributed in countries throughout the world.

Researchers who have examined the link between price controls and innovation in the pharmaceutical industry find that the more stringent a country is in regulating prices, the less successful its domestic pharmaceutical industry is in developing innovative drugs. In Europe, France has among the lowest medicine prices and the tightest regulations, and its home-based drug firms have performed poorly in terms of innovation. Firms based in the United Kingdom have excelled in developing globally innovative drugs, but not nearly as well as U.S. firms. Britain's drug regulatory scheme scrutinizes the "rate of return" by the drug makers, but leaves them free to price individual products as they like. The United States, of course, offers the closest to a free market for prescription drugs of all countries. Even though there is a worldwide market for most highly innovative drugs, home-based firms often fare disproportionately well in selling their own products to their domestic markets. So, when a pharmaceutical company is forced to sell large volumes of its product at low prices at home, it sacrifices revenues that it could plough back into developing new, innovative drugs.[15]

Some countries are known to tie their decision-making about drug approvals and drug prices to commitments from pharmaceutical firms to engage in "economic development" for the nation's sake. We've heard, for instance, that the first "official" case of depression in France was recorded only after a company with an innovative depression drug promised to open a research center in that country that would employ 2,000 people.

The key point here is that a country with high drug prices can *afford* to be the most innovative, at least in accord with how pharmaceutical companies decide to invest in new drugs—which raises one of the most daunting challenges to solving the problem of high prices. And there is no denying that today the United States is the intellectual center for worldwide pharmaceutical and biotechnology R & D. The two largest biotech clusters in the Boston area and around the San Francisco Bay are homes for major research centers of big European drug firms, including AstraZeneca, Novartis, and Roche. Other large European-based multinationals, including Bayer, Boehringer Ingelheim, and Sanofi-Aventis, also have research facilities in the northeastern United States. The world's leading drug manufacturers know that they need to be in the United States to take advantage of the advances that come from the world's leading biomedical research infrastructure.

These large, multinational pharmaceutical firms account for only part of the story of today's innovative drug exploration and development. University laboratories—some of which are funded with your tax dollars—and small biotech firms are a significant and growing source of new drug candidates, too. Taken as a whole, all these biotech firms have sales that add up to those of only one or two of the biggest pharmaceutical firms. But the importance of these small companies as sources for new molecules that could become new drugs has greater significance, and they factor into the overall challenge of how to solve the problem of high drug prices without stifling innovation.

The bottom line is that drug prices in the United States are very high—higher than nearly anywhere else in the world. The United States also leads the world in biotechnology and its tangible outputs—innovative drug molecules, as well as the prestige and economic benefits that accompany them. The profits from high drug prices fuel U.S. innovation by financing the development of new drugs. The whole system appears to hinge on charging high prices—a situation we can no longer endure.

*The bottom line is that drug prices in the United States are very high— higher than nearly anywhere else in the world.*

# *What to Do?*

There is no question that we need to maintain the stream of innovative drugs that has benefited so many people over the past twenty-five years. Putting the brakes on innovation would adversely affect advances toward new therapies for disorders such as Parkinson's disease, Alzheimer's disease, and many forms of cancer. And then there are the overwhelming medical needs of underserved populations, including indigent people in the industrialized countries and people in the developing world.

After seeing a bumper crop of new medicine introductions late in the twentieth century, there appears to be a drought in recent years. The FDA and other drug regulatory agencies in the world have been approving relatively fewer new molecular entities of so-called *small molecule drugs*—the ones with the greatest potential to become blockbusters—because the applications are not forthcoming. Between 1996 and 2000, approvals averaged 37 each year, while between 2001 and 2005 the annual average had fallen to 24. One explanation is, of course, that the scientific challenges of developing new drugs for still unmet medical needs is very difficult. But the industry acknowledges that the tremendously expensive and resource-intensive drug development process plays a big role.[16]

The current approach of financing drug development with revenues earned from members of the population who are sick leads to lots of satisfied patients, but plenty of dissatisfied customers, too. Some of you are helping to finance new drug development even though you're deriving no benefit from the medicines you take. It sounds like exploitation—and some critics use that very word to describe the current state of affairs with the drug industry. Clearly, we need a new way to finance drug development.

As described in brief above, scientific advancements are already facilitating the development of new drugs tailored to specific molecular or genetic characteristics of the pool of patients for whom they will be prescribed. Soon, it will be possible to predict whether a drug will be effective, or non-toxic, but only for much smaller population segments than targeted with blockbuster drugs. Unless something changes, targeting small populations means that prices will go up even more—according to the premium-pricing model. Who will have access to these needed medicines?

There must be a way to lower drug prices while encouraging the continued stream of innovative therapies that characterized the therapeutic revolution of the twentieth century. Can it be found somewhere within the pharmaceutical industry itself? Let's look next at how the industry is structured and how it works.

## *Endnotes*

[1] Shryock, Richard H. 1936. *The Development of Modern Medicine, an Interpretation of the Social and Scientific Factors Involved*. Philadelphia: University of Pennsylvania Press. See also: Temin, Peter. 1980. *Taking Your Medicine: Drug Regulation in the United States*. Cambridge: Harvard University Press.

[2] Cooper, Joseph D., ed. 1970. *The Economics of Drug Innovation*. Washington, D.C.: American University, Center for the Study of Private Enterprise. See also: Holmstedt, Bo and Goren Liljestrand, eds. 1963. *Readings in Pharmacology.* New York: Macmillan.

[3] Surowiecki, J. 2001. No profit, no cure. *New Yorker* Nov. 5:46. See also: McKeown, Thomas, and C. R. Lowe. 1967. *An Introduction to Social Medicine.* Philadelphia: F. A. Davis.

[4] Sinclair, Upton. 1906. *The Jungle*. New York: Doubleday, Page, and Co. See also: Wilson, Stephen. 1942. *Food and Drug Regulation*. Washington, D.C.: American Council on Public Affairs.

[5] Cavers, D. F. 1939. The Food, Drug, and Cosmetic Act of 1938: Its legislative history and its substantive provision. *Law and Contemporary Problems* 6 (Winter): 2–42.

[6] Hopkins, Richard J. 1965. Medical prescriptions and the law: A study of the enactment of the Durham-Humphrey Amendment to the FDC Act. M.A. thesis, Emory University. See also: U.S. House of Representatives. 1951. *Amending Section 503(b) of the Federal Food, Drug, and Cosmetic Act*. H. Rep. 700. 82nd Cong., 1st sess. See also: Marks, H. M. 1995. Revisiting "The origins of compulsory drug prescriptions." *American Journal of Public Health* 85(1): 109–115.

[7] Higgs, Robert. 1995. Wrecking Ball: FDA regulation of medical devices. August 7. www.cato.org/pubs/pas/pa-235.html (accessed April 19, 2007). See also: Mossinghoff, G. 1999. Overview of the Hatch-Waxman Act and its impact on the drug development process. *Food and Drug Law Journal* 54(2): 187–94.

[8] Avorn, J. 1982. Scientific versus commercial sources of influence on the prescribing behavior of physicians. *American Journal of Medicine* 73(1): 4–8.

[9] Radley, D. C. et al. 2006. Off-label prescribing among office-based physicians. *Archive of Internal Medicine* 166:1021–26.

[10] Temin, 1980, *op. cit.*

[11] Marmor, Theodore. 2000. *The Politics of Medicare.* 2nd ed. New York: Aldine de Gruyter.

[12] Waugh, Frederick V. 1929. Quality as a determinant of vegetable prices: A statistical study of qualitative factors influencing vegetable prices in the Boston wholesale market. In *Studies in History, Economics, and Public Law* 312, first AMS edition 1968 (from the Columbia University 1929 Edition). New York: AMS Press.

[13] Berndt, E. R., R. S. Pindyck and P. Azoulay. 1999. Network effects and diffusion in pharmaceutical markets: Antiulcer drugs. NBER Working Paper Series No. 7024 (March). www.nber.org/papers/w7024.pdf (accessed April 19, 2007). See also: Berndt, E. R. and N. J. Rappaport. 2001. Price and quality of desktop and mobile personal computers: A quarter century historical overview. *American Economic Review* 91(2): 268–73. See also: Raff, D. M. G. and M. Trajtenberg. 1995. Quality-adjusted prices for the American automobile industry: 1906–1940. NBER Working Paper No. W5035 (February). http://ssrn.com/abstract=225814.

[14] Bandow, D. 2005. Saving pfennige, costing lives. *Wall Street Journal Europe* (March 16). www.cato.org/pub_display.php?pub_id=3710 (accessed April 19, 2007).

[15] Danzon, Patricia M. 1997. *Pharmaceutical Price Regulation.* Washington, D. C.: The AEI Press.

[16] For 1996 to 2000, average NME approvals found by averaging new molecular entity approvals each year, located in: U.S. Food and Drug Administration. *CDER 2000 Report to the Nation: Improving Public Health Through Human Drugs.* Rockville, Maryland, 2001: p. 8. Available: www.fda.gov/cder/reports/RTN2000/Rtn2000.pdf (accessed May 15, 2007). For 2001 to 2005, average NME approvals found by averaging new molecular entity approvals each year, after adding priority and standard NME approvals (numbers are consistent with 1996 to 2005 averages, 2004 and 2005 numbers include BLA's), located in: U.S. Food and Drug Administration. *CDER 2005 Report to the Nation: Improving Public Health Through Human Drugs.* Rockville, Maryland. 2005: pp. 15 and 17. Available: www.fda.gov/cder/reports/rtn/2005/rtn2005.pdf (accessed May 15, 2007).

# CHAPTER THREE

## THE DRUG INDUSTRY TODAY

*It is easy to get a thousand prescriptions, but hard
to get one single remedy.*

—Chinese proverb

The form and structure of the modern pharmaceutical industry
has a lot to do with high drug prices. The ways in which marketing
and sales of drugs have evolved are as much a result of government
regulation as they are of the progress of science and technology over
the decades. Let's look at how drug companies have evolved since
World War II to the way they do business today. Then we'll explore
how their drug discovery and development processes have changed.

The pharmaceutical industry and the U.S. government are closely
entwined, and the industry—particularly since the 1960s—works
diligently to develop and influence government rules on safety, efficacy,
and marketing to its advantage. Lobbyists for the major drug
companies are no strangers to the halls of power in Washington, and
political contributions from the industry fuel elections from coast to
coast. And why not? The fortunes of the pharmaceutical industry are
tied closely to what government does, and the high earnings of drug
companies make these investments in political influence possible.

As described earlier, the U.S. government's involvement with
medications goes back to the 1906 *Pure Food and Drugs Act*. But it
was during the Great Depression that federal regulation of the drug

industry began to make a significant mark. The New Deal philosophy that industries need regulation to operate properly had a direct impact on drug companies. In 1933, Congress saw a first draft of what eventually became the 1938 *Federal Food, Drug, and Cosmetic Act,* one of many so-called "Second New Deal" measures designed to lift the United States out of its economic woes. Although the bill repeatedly came up for a vote, it always failed to muster enough support. It took yet another drug disaster to propel it to passage.

German scientists researching dyestuffs discovered *sulfanilamide,* an antibiotic, more or less by accident. Aspirin had come about in much the same way many years earlier. But sulfanilamide pills were unpalatable. So, in 1937, the U.S. pharmaceutical company S.E. Massengill introduced a liquid form. As mentioned earlier, the company dissolved the drug in *diethylene glycol*—more commonly known as antifreeze.[1]

Like all non-narcotic drugs at the time, sulfanilamide was available without a prescription. Anyone could buy it. And 100 people died from this toxin in one of the worst cases of adverse drug reactions in history.

Congress didn't want another sulfanilamide-like disaster, but the FDA lacked the authority to act. So in 1938, Congress set out to make self-medication safer, stipulating that drugs be labeled either with an explanation about how they could be used safely or with some indication that they were safe to use "By Prescription Only." The drug companies themselves were allowed to choose which label they'd use. But a newly empowered FDA interpreted the law its own way and decided to limit drug availability with "By Prescription Only" labels.

You might think that sounds bad for drug sales. In fact, a big commercial opportunity was created. Selling *dangerous*—that is, powerful—drugs only by prescription allowed drug companies to slash their advertising budgets. They didn't need to reach vast numbers of consumers, but could focus their marketing on doctors. As researchers discovered new drugs after the start of World War II, including antibiotics that improved on sulfanilamide, this direct-to-physicians approach served the industry quite well. This model was used for a very long time, until the industry shifted gears in the 1980s and pushed instead for direct-to-consumer advertising.

## Antibiotics Spawn a New Industry

The pharmaceutical industry today owes its very existence to the "new" antibiotics. Penicillin was the first and greatest of these. Isolated in 1929, it was made into a potent drug during World War II, and by war's end had completely supplanted sulfa drugs as the treatment of choice for battle injuries. In 1944, some nineteen U.S. companies produced penicillin; the largest five accounted for nearly 90 percent of the total. Only one of these five was *vertically integrated*—that is, combined the manufacturing, packaging, and sales of drugs.

After the war, as the business climate transformed into what became boom years, antibiotics were a very attractive business proposition for drug companies. In 1944, Selman Waxman of Rutgers University discovered streptomycin, and it wasn't long after that scientists—and profit-seeking drug companies—realized that penicillin was just the beginning of

*Since World War II, the pharmaceutical industry has become one of the strongest and most profitable industries in U.S. history.*

a spate of antibiotic "wonder drugs." It was a turning point for what has since become one of the strongest and most profitable industries in U.S. history.

Waxman's discovery was especially promising because his method—screening soil samples for the presence of agents that kept soil relatively harmless—could be generalized. It was icing on the cake when it turned out that streptomycin could be patented; even though the underlying antibiotic occurred naturally, the patent office ruled that the refinement and packaging of the drug had led to a "new composition of matter." This meant companies using Waxman's method could make other proprietary discoveries—and, of course, any new drugs resulting from the discoveries could be labeled as "By Prescription Only" and marketed directly to doctors.

Prior to World War II, nearly all drug companies had formulated medicines and furnished them in bulk to doctors and pharmacists. Under the new regulations, existing drug companies and new entrants saw a way to increase profits and jumped at the chance to build vertically integrated firms that would discover, produce, package, promote, and sell new drugs in finished form to doctors. As they integrated forward from manufacturing into marketing, new technologies encouraged them to integrate backward into drug research and development. The modern pharmaceutical company, as you know it, dates from these early postwar years.

R & D spending grew, as did marketing. A race ensued to discover new drugs. Patents did their job, restricting competition and thus encouraging more innovation. Sometimes, companies combined to avoid patent fights. Business boomed. The share of prescription drugs in pharmacy sales rose from nearly 10 percent in 1940 to 40 percent a quarter-century later, and the proportion of drugs packaged in their final form by their actual manufacturers also increased dramatically.

Meanwhile, direct advertising to doctors, called *detailing*, grew and intensified. Drug companies sent representatives, called *detail men*, to visit doctors personally and urge them to use the new drugs. They left behind the pens, pads of paper, magnets, and drug samples you've seen at their offices. The main producers of new antibiotics spent more than half of their advertising dollars on detailing in the 1950s, and doctors received most of their information about new drugs from detail men.

The market power of the pharmaceutical industry was on the rise, as reflected by profits. But consumers, simply amazed at the new wonder drugs, didn't seem to mind. After all, these drugs saved lives. They were even cheap compared to a stay in the hospital. Some politicians in Washington, though, did begin to stir, upset at the high profits of the new, vertically integrated drug companies. Prices were just starting to attract government attention.

In the early 1960s, Senator Estes Kefauver held widely publicized hearings on the drug industry. His particular concern: "He who orders does not buy, and he who buys does not order." This fact made the demand for drugs insensitive to price, since doctors didn't care about the price and patients had no choice among prescription drugs. No wonder companies' profits were high: even if prices rose, sales volume would remain fairly constant.[2]

Kefauver introduced a bill to reduce the drug companies' market power, but it became so diluted in committee that he refused to manage his own bill through debate on the Senate floor. Then came thalidomide (mentioned in Chapter 2, "The American Way to Discover Drugs"). This new drug disaster changed the political climate and propelled new legislation into law, just as it happened with sulfanilamide in 1938. But rather than address Kefauver's aim of curbing the market power of pharmaceutical companies, the 1962 *Drug Amendments* rewrote the standards for approving new drugs. In doing so, the new law cemented the intimate relationship between the government and the industry.

It used to be that safety—the issue in both the sulfanilamide and thalidomide disasters—was the sole standard for drug approval. The 1962 law expanded the standard to include efficacy, the ability of the drug to produce a desired effect. Three important changes in the relationship between pharmaceutical companies and the FDA resulted.

1. Drugs would now be sold only if the FDA actively approved a company's New Drug Application (NDA), instead of simply not objecting.

2. The FDA had new authority over testing of new drugs, which had to be done in accord with its guidelines.

3. Firms had to get FDA permission to initiate testing in humans.

The 1962 law applied not just to new drugs, but also those already on the market, which had to be brought up to the new standards. Committees met throughout the 1960s to review all drugs, with the FDA authorized to remove from the market any that failed to measure up to the new standards.

The 1938 regulations had inserted doctors between consumers and their medicines; the 1962 amendments put the FDA between doctors and the drugs they prescribed. It wasn't much longer before the FDA's mark on the production and marketing of *all* drugs was evident. And the 1962 law also created the conditions for today's blockbuster mentality. By making it much easier for generic manufacturers to enter the market, the law showed pharmaceutical companies that they needed to maximize revenues while they still enjoyed patent protection. Companies realized over time that this would require a new marketing approach, because detailing only got so far in motivating doctors to prescribe their drugs. What if drug companies could get patients (and potential patients) to exert influence on doctors, too?

## *Creating a "Sales Force" of Consumers*

A shift began in 1981. The pharmaceutical industry began to urge the FDA to allow direct-to-consumer (DTC) advertising, citing the "educational" benefits—despite research questioning whether drug companies beholden to shareholders rather than patients would substitute increased sales for consumer safety. Then some companies decided to see how far they could push against existing FDA rules. Eli Lilly & Co. embarked on an aggressive advertising campaign for its arthritis drug *Oraflex*. Spectacular sales resulted, but the FDA reprimanded Lilly for "misleading information" in its ads. Pfizer was accused of omitting adverse reactions in ads for its angina medication *Procardia*. Meanwhile, physicians began to report that they felt pressured by patients to prescribe drugs the doctors didn't think were needed.[3]

FDA Commissioner Dr. Arthur Hull Hayes asked drug companies for a voluntary moratorium on their ads. Speaking in 1983 to the Pharmaceutical Advertising Council, his message, in essence, was stop *pushing* us on the issue and the FDA will seriously consider revising its regulations. That set off a lot of back-and-forth arguing. The industry claimed Hayes himself had incited the ad campaigns with his enthusiastic and optimistic statements in an earlier speech to the same group. Hayes retorted that he had simply hoped to encourage educational campaigns, not blatant advertising for drugs. Soon other groups chimed in: the American Medical Association (AMA) expressed concerns and the AARP declared its readiness to lobby Congress for an outright ban on DTC advertising.[4]

All this unfolded amidst the Reagan administration's deregulation fervor, and by 1985 a notice in the Federal Register stated that existing advertising guidelines were sufficient, silently ending the moratorium. However, the back-and-forth continued: The FDA insisted its regulations protected consumers from misleading advertisements, while drug companies argued that the required "summaries" of risks meant so many extra pages of print or TV commercial time that it made advertising impossible. All the while, some drug companies continued to frustrate the FDA with ads that pushed the envelope. You've probably seen some of these ads on television. They use implied imagery to convey a drug's purpose without naming the product outright, all designed to get you to ask your doctor whether you "need" it. The most prevalent ad promoted the "Purple Pill."[5]

Business is business, and no one was shocked when the broadcast networks, hungry for advertising profits, joined the pharmaceutical industry's efforts to change FDA policy. In 1985, CBS announced its intention to broadcast "responsible" prescription-drug commercials (although none aired until 1989). Meanwhile, the FDA was fighting back, accusing Upjohn in 1986 of misleading the public with its claim that *Rogaine*, a treatment for baldness, stopped hair loss or made hair grow. Other companies tried to stay within the guidelines; for example, ads for the birth-control pill N.E.E. 1/35 ran without FDA objection because they never specified the drug's purpose.[6]

In late 1989, the Prescription Drug Advertisement Coalition—composed of 14 major pharmaceutical companies and representatives from ABC, CBS, and NBC—upped the ante, lobbying the FDA to allow the networks to run ads for four popular prescription drugs in a test market. At the same time, CBS and ABC broadcast Nicorette commercials that named the prescription drug.[7]

The debate intensified. Doctors and healthcare advocates condemned the industry for its so-called "educational" initiatives. When a new FDA commissioner came on board, he announced in 1991 plans to double the size of the FDA's promotion and advertising division and up the ante yet again. Dr. David A. Kessler even threatened drug companies with injunctions and prosecution instead of letters of warning, the usual first step by the FDA in its enforcement process (which can ultimately lead to the seizure of drugs by the agency). And in a 1993 letter to pharmaceutical companies, he requested a voluntary submission of all advertisements for FDA review before releasing them to the public.[8]

A public hearing on DTC advertising followed in 1995. Pharmaceutical and advertising representatives came out in force to press for a change in policy.[9] In 1997, after Kessler had stepped down, the FDA gave in: A drug's name and the condition it treated could be included in advertisements without the need to disclose every risk (a policy that was finalized in 1999). Drug companies and broadcasters hailed the greater "consumer awareness" would result. Why did the FDA change its position? Part of the answer surely has to do with the real debate over the benefits and detriments of DTC advertising. But another is clearly the relentless pressure from those with a financial interest in relaxing the regulations. As one pharmaceutical industry analyst stated, "Advertising directly to consumers is one of the most successful movements ever in the pharmaceuticals industry. It is the product of advertising executives all over America who went to sleep each night trying to figure out how to sell prescription drugs to the public without upsetting the apple cart at the FDA."[10]

Consumer rights groups were outraged by the FDA's decision (even if consumers seemed to pay little attention). Advertisements for prescription drugs skyrocketed. Pharmaceutical industry spending doubled to $2.5 billion between 1997 and 2000 and reached $4.2 billion by 2004. Prescription drug advertising is now ubiquitous on television and in the print media. And consumers took the bait: A 1998 national survey revealed "33 percent of those who have seen such ads have spoken to their doctors about an advertised drug. Of those consumers, 28 percent asked for prescriptions—and 80 percent of such requests were granted." Profits swelled: Each dollar spent on ads produced an additional $4.20 in sales. The industry's pressure on the FDA clearly paid off.[11] No wonder it's impossible to turn on your television today without being barraged by advertisements for blockbuster—or potential blockbuster—prescription drugs like Nexium or Lipitor.

> *It's impossible to turn on your television today without being barraged by advertisements for blockbuster—or potential blockbuster—prescription drugs.*

The success of DTC advertising in generating revenue for pharmaceutical companies is very good news for an industry that is now suffering from a relative dearth of new products to sell. The number of drugs receiving final FDA approval has hit a stagnation point, and the industry is not quite sure what to do. There's still a steady growth in the number of *Investigational New Drug (IND) applications* submitted to the FDA (reaching 2,374 in 2002); that's the petition submitted to the FDA to allow testing of a new drug in clinical trials. But approval of *New Drug Applications (NDAs)*—the request to market the drug after clinical trials are completed—for New Molecular Entities (NMEs) has fallen from a peak of 53 in 1996 to only 17 in 2005.[12]

## *Manipulating Patients?*

With such a low probability of launching a drug candidate onto the market successfully, it didn't sit well with drug companies when researchers began to show a "dark side" to DTC—namely, that it manipulates the way patients think about medicines—soon after the ads began to run. The industry countered with contrary findings. This dueling research (see sidebar) has only fueled the debate.[13]

More recently, controversies over several drugs—and, ultimately, their recall—have widened the skepticism of consumers targeted by DTC advertising. In October 2004, Merck recalled its arthritis drug *Vioxx*, which the company had been promoting aggressively with DTC advertising since 1998. Some 2 million people had Vioxx prescriptions. Only later was it discovered that COX-2 inhibitors such as Vioxx increase the risk of heart attack and stroke in patients; an outstanding question is whether drug firms knew this before their medicines hit the market. In April 2005, Pfizer pulled its similar drug, Bextra.

### DUELING RESEARCH ON DTC

The first research findings issued after the FDA changed its guidelines found that DTC advertising decreases the effectiveness of physicians to treat patients thoroughly, and doctors report that they felt increased pressure from their patients to prescribe new drugs. While lauding ads that prompt patients who previously felt isolated and embarrassed about a condition to ask for treatment, most doctors admit to feeling pressured by their patients to prescribe drugs. While few people visit their doctors exclusively because of a prescription drug campaign, the ads often motivate them to discuss medical problems with their doctor. In a 2004 study, approximately 80 percent of physicians felt that DTC advertising "did not provide information in a balanced manner" and "encouraged patients to seek treatments they did not need." Many doctors describe brainwashed patients who treat an office visit like a trip to the grocery store, convinced that a drug seen on television is the best and only medication for something they may not even have. Most worrisome to doctors, though, was a patient survey that showed 15 percent of consumers would "consider switching doctors if they didn't get a drug they specifically asked for." [14]

And what do consumers say? Some have benefited as DTC ads remind them to take their medicine or refill prescriptions. Some 67 percent describe feeling better educated about their drug choices, although 61 percent are confused by the ads. A year after an advertising campaign for an osteoporosis drug, the number of women consulting physicians about the disease doubled. A researcher at Massachusetts General Hospital was told by patients that drug advertising would primarily cause them to discuss allergy, arthritis, and cholesterol-lowering drugs with their doctors. But when doctors were asked what drug advertising caused patients to ask the most questions, they identified impotence pills. [15]

Other research presented to the FDA in September 2003 claimed DTC did *not* dramatically affect doctors, insisting that only a few "consider it a significant problem." In a survey of 500 physicians, 41 percent said drug advertising had positive aspects, while 18 percent found it to be significantly problematic. The FDA's own 2003 study found aggressive campaigning lead to 7 percent of general practitioners feeling "very pressured" to prescribe heavily advertised drugs, with 6 percent saying it had a "very negative effect on their practice." Another study determined that less than 30 percent of doctors think DTC advertising is a positive trend and 67 percent expressed concern that patients' expectations of doctor's prescribing practices were changing. A more bizarre study, involving actresses pretending to be victims of adjustment disorder, found doctors were five times more likely to write prescriptions for the antidepressant Paxil when its TV commercial was mentioned to them—even when the symptoms didn't call for medication.[16]

The bottom line is a significant level of complaints from doctors about DTC advertising. As one Denver-area doctor said in 2001, "I do not find it helpful. It shows the drug companies for what they are— profiteers. [Education is] not the reason they do it, and that's not the way it really works."[17]

The FDA narrowly voted to allow the drugs back on the market under strict conditions in February 2005, but Rodale, which publishes on health and wellness topics, found "increased reservations among consumers" who began paying less attention to the benefits of advertised drugs. When consumers scrutinize the side effects and warnings more thoroughly, it makes DTC advertising less effective. As drug companies faced bad press and Vioxx-related lawsuits accusing Merck of hiding information from consumers, pharmaceutical companies softened their ads and imposed self-governing restrictions in June 2005. Optional guidelines were created to limit DTC advertising during the first year after a product came onto the market, allowing doctors more time to study a product before their patients began requesting it.[18]

So, the controversy over DTC rages on at the same time that "ask your doctor" has become as familiar a phrase in advertising as "I can't believe I ate the whole thing" from an earlier era.

## Another Approach to Selling Prescription Drugs

Direct-to-consumer (DTC) advertising may have helped keep drug companies highly profitable, but it addresses only part of the challenge. Once a drug has been discovered and produced, and after consumers and their physicians are made aware of its availability, the drug still needs to be in the hands of end users. Could a mechanism for dealing with the insurance companies and governments that pay for the drugs be as beneficial for the pharmaceutical industry as DTC advertising has been with the general public? How might the industry do as good a job of getting pharmacies to stock their products?

Traditionally, drug manufacturers sold their products to a few wholesalers, who in turn would be the middlemen that sold to many small, independent retail pharmacies. The new model involves a *Pharmacy Benefit Manager (PBM)*, who acts as a middleman between the drug companies and those who *ultimately* pay for the bulk of prescription medications. The pharmaceutical industry likes to cite studies done by the Federal Trade Commission (FTC), Government Accounting Office, and others that find PBMs help to expand access, promote quality, and, most important, reduce the cost of prescription drugs to consumers by upwards of 27 percent.[19]

How does this serve the interests of the pharmaceutical industry? The answer: not directly, but still quite substantially.

Here's how PBMs work. They leverage their size and the number of people they represent to negotiate discounts as much as 18 percent for brand-name drugs, and 47 percent for generic drugs, while still providing employers and their insurers with attractive *formularies* (lists of the medicines that a drug-plan will agree to pay for) that include drugs in most therapeutic categories. PBMs also reduce costs by substituting generic drugs for a brand-name drug when appropriate. Furthermore, PBMs are eligible for manufacturer rebates based on their purchases, which can reduce their drug spending by 3 to 9 percent. PBMs also cut costs with their mail-service pharmacies for the insured, offering brand-name drugs at prices 27 percent lower and generic drugs at prices 53 percent lower than the average price paid at retail pharmacies.[20]

The government certainly believes in PBMs, claims the Pharmaceutical Care Management Association (the PBM industry group). The association points to the *Medicare Modernization Act* of 2003, which stipulates that PBMs take a major role in the funded Medicare prescription drug benefit (more on this in Chapter 5, "How *Not* to Lower Drug Prices"). The PBMs claim they can reduce Medicare drug costs by up to 30 percent.[21]

All of these seemingly straightforward benefits mask another picture. In the words of well-known commentator Ben Stein, to be a PBM means making money "by denying benefits of various kinds, especially prescriptions, to patients and employees, thus supposedly saving money for employers and keeping a big chunk of that money for itself."[22] And while Stein acknowledges the statement as an "oversimplification" but "basically true," more and more employers and pharmacies believe that PBMs have shied away from their original role as middlemen, transforming into unethical, profit-hungry organizations focused more on their own gain than on lowering drug costs for their clients. In the course of this transformation, they have become tied more closely to the big pharmaceutical companies. Are the PBMs and drug companies colluding to set prices?[23]

The first among several problems is that PBMs lack transparency, which fuels suspicion that the drug companies themselves benefit from PBMs. But how could the drug companies benefit when they discount their prices for their PBM buyers? *Market share*. PBMs have grown so big that they now have the power to manipulate a drug manufacturer's market share by persuading health plans to choose a particular drug. In return, the manufacturer offers the health plan a rebate. Details of these rebates are not disclosed to the health plan, and the PBMs keep a large portion—up to 25 percent, on top of the fee PBMs collect from the health plans they serve.[24]

The problems don't end with the lack of transparency. The PBM business also creates an absence of competition. Three PBMs— Medco Health Solutions, Caremark Rx, and Express-Scripts, Inc.— control 80 to 90 percent of the PBM market. In addition, some accuse PBMs of profiting from the sale of drugs to their clients at a much higher price than they pay for them from manufacturers. And on top of rebates in general, there's the question of whether PBMs receive special incentives from drug companies to promote more expensive drugs. Just as a PBM may substitute a generic for a brand-name drug in its formulary, it can also substitute a more expensive drug for a cheaper equivalent if the drug company provides enough of an incentive. Even with the discounted prices, the health plan would end up incurring a greater cost.[25]

The major PBMs have an interesting way of dealing with these accusations. Medco Health Solutions, the nation's largest PBM, paid Massachusetts $5.5 million to settle allegations that the company kept millions of dollars from drug company rebates rather than passing the money on to the state. When 20 states and the federal government combined to accuse Medco of violating consumer protection and mail fraud laws, it arranged a $29.3 million settlement agreement.[26] These lawsuits raise the specter of whether PBMs do honest business. No wonder several state legislatures, including Maine, South Dakota, and the District of Columbia, have passed laws requiring greater PBM transparency through fiduciary and disclosure provisions. On another front, employers have formed coalitions to require their chosen PBMs to pass on 100 percent of rebates and discounts they get from manufacturers to member companies. And still other employers have brought their rebate management services in-house or developed worksite pharmacies. Some insurers have also gotten into the PBM business on their own behalf.[27]

The mail-order aspect of PBMs is also extremely controversial. IMS Health (a leading source of pharmaceutical market data) estimates that drugs ordered by mail, the fastest-growing sales channel for prescription drugs, grew 18 percent in 2004 to $33.9 billion. That accounts for 14.4 percent of the total U.S. prescription drug market. Since mail-order pharmacies are highly automated and require little building space or staff, they have an edge over retail pharmacies. The PBMs can fill and mail a prescription for $2.50—a fraction of what it would cost at a retail store. How does that translate into savings? If all employees of the state of Ohio that use Express Scripts' mail-order facility were to purchase their drugs at a retail store, their annual cost of prescription drugs would rise to $62 million from the current $50 million.[28]

These changes are contributing to the disappearance of the independent pharmacy, now nearly extinct from neighborhoods across the United States. Independent druggists sold a third of all prescription drugs in the early 1990s; today they sell half that amount. The big pharmacy chains have a lot to do with that, but mail order has doubled over the last decade, from less than 10 percent of sales in the mid-1990s to roughly double that now. The pharmacy chain CVS recently purchased Caremark Rx, one of the largest PBMs. It is too early to tell how this might change the competitive landscape.

According to the Coalition for Quality Healthcare, PBMs set artificially low rates on their mail-order drugs to drive business in their direction. Many PBMs also require their clients' employees to purchase 90-day supplies of maintenance medications (e.g., Lipitor for high cholesterol) by mail. These maintenance drugs make up about 60 percent of the retail prescription drug market and retail stores complain that this requirement is stealing away even more of their pharmacy customers. Several large pharmacy chains are fighting back by creating PBM branches of their own,[29] but whether this will create sorely needed competition is uncertain.[30] As the pharmaceutical companies continue to reap big profits, run

*As the pharmaceutical companies continue to reap big profits, run their ads directed at you (the consumer), embrace PBMs, and spend millions to influence decision-makers in Washington, the prices for drugs continue to rise.*

their ads directed at you (the consumer), embrace PBMs, and spend millions to influence decision-makers in Washington, the prices for drugs continue to rise. At nearly every juncture, when the issue of price is raised the industry repeats the same mantra about its *risk*. Let's look more closely at what role risk might play in the price you pay for drugs.

## *Endnotes*

[1] The need for ongoing regulation is shown by a new problem with diethylene glycol. Bogdanich, W. and R. McLean. 2007. Poisoned toothpaste in Panama is believed to be from China. *New York Times*, May 19.

[2] U.S. Senate. 1961. *Administered Prices, Drugs.* S. Res. 448, 3. 87th Cong., 1st sess.

[3] Altman, L. K. 1982. The doctor's world. *New York Times*, August 17. See also: Russell, C. 1982. Drug ads regulation increased. *Washington Post*, September 8. See also: Wilkes, M., R. Bell, and R. Kravitz. 2000. Direct-to-consumer prescription drug advertising: Trends, impact, and implication. *Health Affairs* 19(2): 110–28.

[4] Staff Reporter. 1983. FDA chief opposes prescription drug ads to consumer, for now. *Wall Street Journal*, February 18. See also: Hinds, M. 1983. Prescription drug ads: Direct dose to consumers. *New York Times*, May 29. See also: Waldholz, M. 1983. Consumer drug ads may soon run as FDA considers drafting rules. *Wall Street Journal*. February 17.

[5] U.S. FDA. 1985. Direct to Consumer Advertising of Prescription Drugs; Withdrawal of Moratorium. *Federal Register* 50 (9 September): 36677. See also: Rosenthal, E. 1991. Drug makers set off a bitter debate with ads aimed directly at patients. *New York Times*, March 3. See also: Wilkes, Bell, and Kravitz, *op. cit.*

[6] Crudele, J. 1986. FDA questions Upjohn statement. *New York Times*, June 18:D4. See also: Deutsch, C. 1989. The brouhaha over drug ads. *New York Times*, May 14. See also: Lipman, J. 1989. Drug firm aims to put the pill on TV. *Wall Street Journal*, June 12:B6. See also: Morrow, D. 1998. Spending it: From lab to patient, by way of your den. *New York Times*, June 7.

[7] Gladwell, M. and P. Farhi. 1990. Drug firms offering new prescription for TV ads. *Washington Post*, January 28:H1. See also: Rothenberg, R. 1989. CBS and ABC to use ad that names drug. *New York Times*, December 18:D11.

[8] U.S. Department of Health and Human Services. 2005. Consumer-directed promotion of regulated medical products; public hearing. *Federal Register* 70(176). www.fda.gov/ohrms/dockets/98fr/05-18040.htm (accessed April 19, 2007). See also: Rosenthal, E., *op. cit.*

[9] A 1996 notice in the Federal Register addresses some of the issues brought up by the hearing, specifically reiterating that the 1993 request for pre-approval was not a legal requirement and soliciting further information from interested parties. U.S. FDA. 1996b. Direct-to-Consumer Promotion. *Federal Register* 61(94) (14 May), 24314.

[10] U.S. FDA. 1995. Direct-to-Consumer Promotion; Public Hearing. *Federal Register* 60 (16 August), 42581. See also: Elliott, S. 1998. A seminar examines the plethora of prescription drug pitches since regulations were loosened. *New York Times,* June 15:D11. See also: U.S. FDA. 1999. Guidance for industry: Consumer-directed broadcast advertisements. www.fda.gov/cder/guidance/1804fnl.htm (accessed April 19, 2007). See also: U.S. FDA. 1999. Guidance for industry: consumer-directed broadcast advertisements questions and answers. www.fda.gov/cder/guidance/1804q&a.htm (accessed April 19, 2007). See also: Morrow, D. 1998. *op. cit.* See also: Stout, D. 1997. Drug makers get leeway on TV ads. *New York Times,* August 9. See also: U.S. FDA. 1996a. Transcript of Direct-to-Consumer Promotion Public Hearing—Oct. 18 & 19, 1995. FDA/Center for Drug Evaluation and Research (April 18, 2006). Available: www.fda.gov/cder/ddmac/meetings.htm.

[11] Elliott, S. 1998a. Take two direct sales pitches for prescription drugs and call your pollster in the morning. *New York Times,* July 29:D5. See also: Ives, N. 2005. Survey says consumers are looking past commercials to study the news about prescription drugs. *New York Times,* March 25:C1. See also: Morrow, D., *op. cit.* See also: Serota, S. 2001. Editorial: Drugs and advertising. *New York Times,* November 28:A24.

[12] U.S. FDA. 2006. Approval times for priority and standard NDAs and BLAs, 1993–2005. May 17. www.fda.gov/cder/rdmt/NDAapps93-05.htm (accessed April 19, 2007). When new Biological License Applications for therapeutic biologic products are included, the number grows to 20 in 2005. See also: Rosenthal, Meredith B., et al. 2002. Promotion of prescription drugs to consumers. *New England Journal of Medicine* 346 (February 14): 498–505.

[13] DiLorenzo, F. 2005. Biotechnology. *Standard and Poor's Industry Surveys* (June 16).

[14] Booth, M. 2001. Drug ads putting pressure on doctors. *Denver Post,* September 16. See also: Kaufman, M. 2003. Drug ads do more good than harm, FDA told. *Washington Post,* September 23. See also: Tanouye, E. 1997. Health Journal: Drug ads spur patients to demand more prescriptions. *Wall Street Journal,* December 22. See also: Weissman J. S., D. Blumenthal, A. J. Silk et al. 2004. Physicians report on patient encounters involving direct-to-consumer advertising. *Health Affairs* (April 28). http://content.healthaffairs.org/cgi/reprint/hlthaff.w4.219v1 (accessed April 19, 2007).

[15] Elliott, S., 1998a, *op. cit.* See also: Holmer, A. 2000. Knowledge is healing. *USA Today,* September 28:16A. See also: Kaufman, M., 2003, *op. cit.*

[16] Kaufman, M., 2003, *ibid.* See also: Kravitz, R. L., R. M. Epstein, et al. 2005. Influence of patients' requests for direct-to-consumer advertised antidepressants:

A randomized controlled trial. *Journal of the American Medical Association* 293(16): 1995–2002. See also: Robinson A. R. and K. B. Hohmann. 2004. Direct-to-consumer pharmaceutical advertising: Physician and public opinion and potential effects on the physician-patient relationship. *Archives of Internal Medicine* 164(4): 427–432.

[17] Booth, M., *op. cit.*

[18] Belli, A. 2005. Verdict reverberates far beyond Merck. *Houston Chronicle*, August 20:A1. See also: Ives, N., *op. cit.* See also: Kaufman, M. 2005. New study criticizes painkiller marketing; arthritis drug ads a factor in overuse. *Washington Post*, January 25:A1. See also: Schmit, J. 2005. Drugmakers likely to lob softer pitches. *USA Today*, March 16:3B. See also: Saul, S. 2005. A self-imposed ban on drug ads. *New York Times*, June 15:C7.

[19] Pharmaceutical Care Management Association, 2005, *op. cit.* See also: U.S. General Accounting Office. 1997. *Pharmacy Benefit Managers: FEHBP plans satisfied with savings and services, but retail pharmacies have concerns*. GAO/HEHS-97-47 (February). Washington, D.C.: U.S. Government Printing Office.

[20] Some PBMs have even started specialty pharmacies that develop clinical techniques for high-cost specialty pharmaceuticals to bring down treatment costs, as well as to encourage electronic prescribing. See: U.S. General Accounting Office. 2003. *Federal Employees' Health Benefits: Effects of Using Pharmacy Benefit Managers on Health Plans, Enrollees, and Pharmacies*. GAO-03-196 (January). Washington, D.C.: U.S. Government Printing Office. www.pcmanet.org/research/ostudies/gaoreport.pdf (accessed April 19, 2007).

[21] Pharmaceutical Care Management Association, 2005, *op. cit.*

[22] Stein, B. 2007. Everybody's business: Shareholders? what shareholders? *New York Times*, January 21.

[23] Freudenheim, M. 2005. Employers unite in effort to curb prescription costs. *New York Times*, February 3:C3. See also: Scanlon, B. 2005. Drug-benefit firms blamed for rising costs; but industry execs say competition keeps prices down. *Rocky Mountain News*, August 4:22A.

[24] Edlin, M. 2004. Plans continue to weigh the debate over direct contracting vs. PBM servicing. *Managed Healthcare Executive* 14:7, 50–51.

[25] Beck, E. 2005. The battle for PBM transparency. *United Press International* (February 3). See also: Wojcik, J. 2005. Drug chain trying another dose of PBM business to compete. *Business Insurance* 39:18, 1.

[26] To ensure cooperation, Medco's practices and dealings are monitored by an independent auditor. In return, the companies pay Medco a negotiated administrative fee. This model is expected to save roughly 6 percent, or $50 million a year, on the group's annual drug costs of $800 million. See: Two Large Employer Coalitions

Insist on Full Transparency in PBM Arrangements. AISHealth. 2005a. *Drug Benefit News*, February 11, 2005.

[27] Touchpoint Health Plan and Dean Health Plan, two physician-owned insurers in Wisconsin, joined forces to create Navitus Health Solutions to manage prescription drug costs. Insuring a total of about 600,000 lives, Navitus saved $3 million in its first two months through drug rebates, compared with $300,000 in the last year from their previous PBM. Mark Huetten, Navitus director of client services, believes that insurers can do better than PBMs when they manage their own formulary, although it does require commitment and resources. One main benefit to a company managing its own drug formulary is that it can focus more on generics and more appropriate drugs, while PBMs tend to pursue major brand-name drugs. See Edlin, 2004, *op. cit*. See also: AISHealth. 2005b. Latest Maine PBM Ruling May Not Bode Well for Industry's Case, Analysts Advise. *Drug Benefit News*, July 15, 2005. See also: Seay, M. 2005. Regulating pharmacy benefit managers with transparency. *Healthcare Financial Management* 59:5, 18.

[28] Boyle, M. 2005. Drug wars. *Fortune* 151:12, 79. See also: Edlin, M. 2005. Gloves come off between retail and mail-order pharmacies. *Managed Healthcare Executive* 15:4, 38.

[29] Walgreen's Health Initiatives, the PBM branch of the major drug store, created its own program called Advantage 90, which offers 90-day prescriptions in the store at the same low cost of mail-order services. This program is now used by more than 150 employers. Walgreen's has also tried to shun the companies that participate in mail-order services, now refusing to fill prescriptions in Ohio, where Express Scripts is the mandatory mail service. Rite-Aid, with its 3,400 stores in 28 states, has recently created its own PBM. Similar to Walgreen's PBM branch, Rite-Aid will also offer the 90-day refill program at all its pharmacies at the same price of mail-order services. John Malley of the pharmacy benefit consulting practice at PriceWaterhouseCoopers believes that Rite-Aid's entrance into the PBM market will stir up competition in the industry. He believes the 90-day in-store refills offer employers something different from the regular PBM services. CVS also has acquired Caremark in another combination of pharmacy and PBM. See: Edlin, *ibid*. See also: Wojcik, 2005, *op. cit*.

[30] Boyle, 2005, *op. cit*.

# CHAPTER FOUR

## ARE DRUG COMPANIES RISKY?

*You'll always miss 100% of the shots you don't take.*

—Wayne Gretzky

Whether it's directly through congressional testimony or subtly in a television advertisement touting America's drug companies, the pharmaceutical industry offers the same reply to the question of why drug prices are so high: Its payback for the risk firms take to create these wonderful, innovative drugs. Knowing what we now do about how the pharmaceuticals business has changed over a century and how the marketplace has shifted, what can we say about this issue of risk?

It *is* true that the process of discovering and developing new drugs is fraught with risk. But does the fact that success with a new molecular entity is risky necessarily translate into *company* risk? Since so much of the discussion focuses on risk and return on the stock markets, examining how drug companies have fared on the market is the next logical step—where *risk* is defined as the chance that the value of an investment could decline.

Investing in stocks is risky because you don't *know* what will happen. Some of your fear is assuaged by paying attention to how a stock has done historically. If you were investing in the early 1980s, Microsoft was a risky proposition. You didn't know how it would do over time. Looking back, we know that there was little risk, and Microsoft stock purchased back then has paid its investors handsomely.

If you know in advance what will perform well in the stock market, you could be as rich as Warren Buffett. It doesn't help only to know later; in retrospect, successful companies always look good. The trick is to pick the right stocks *before* you know their fate.

If the pharmaceutical industry is risky, then trying to predict which company stocks will do well should be difficult. We constructed two portfolios of drug-company stocks to test whether the pharmaceutical industry *is* risky. Each includes the top 10 drug companies, combining different starting points (1973, 1982, and 1997) and sets of companies (starting from the lists in 1973, 1980, and 1997). We then looked at the returns on investing in these stocks in two ways. First, we examined the stocks of the largest companies at the beginning of each period and evaluated how well they did, and then we looked at the largest companies at the end of each period and determined how they did. We know that if the results are different, it's fair to say that the large pharmaceutical companies are risky investments. But if the results are essentially the same, it's equally fair to say that there was no trick to picking which company would succeed—hence, these companies were not investment risks. Basically, you could have invested in any of these stocks and realized a healthy return.

Here's the "small print" for our experiment. Our portfolios are weighted by company sales, so that larger companies have larger shares in the portfolio, and are composed of companies' stocks based on their sales. We calculated the proportion of each company's sales to the top 10 companies' total revenue, and invested this portion of the portfolio in the company's stocks. In the first portfolio, we took the 10 largest companies at the start of the period; in the second, we took the 10 largest companies at the end of the period. We adjusted stocks for mergers. These portfolios, as well as Dow Jones and NYSE composite, are shown in Table 4-1.

TABLE 4-1. *Portfolios Used for Measuring the Risk of Investing in the Pharmaceutical Industry (Top 10 Pharmaceutical Companies by Sales)*

| 1973–1982 | 1973 | 1976 | 1979 | 1982 | | |
|---|---|---|---|---|---|---|
| 1973 S&P 500 | 100.0 | 110.2 | 98.5 | 144.2 | | |
| 1973 Top10 | 100.0 | 72.0 | 64.9 | 82.6 | | |
| 1980 Top10 | 100.0 | 81.9 | 106.7 | 151.5 | | |
| 1997 Top10 | 100.0 | 79.2 | 80.3 | 109.7 | | |
| **1982–1997** | **1982** | **1985** | **1988** | **1991** | **1994** | **1997** |
| 1982 S&P 500 | 100.0 | 150.2 | 197.5 | 296.6 | 326.6 | 690.0 |
| 1973 Top10 | 100.0 | 143.1 | 296.4 | 456.1 | 498.5 | 1008.1 |
| 1980 Top10 | 100.0 | 131.1 | 274.5 | 457.2 | 534.3 | 1103.1 |
| 1997 Top10 | 100.0 | 139.0 | 290.5 | 497.1 | 573.5 | 1186.0 |
| **1997–2005** | **1997** | **2000** | **2003** | **2005** | | |
| 1997 S&P 500 | 100.0 | 136.1 | 114.6 | 117.7 | | |
| 1973 Top10 | 100.0 | 207.6 | 166.9 | 149.2 | | |
| 1980 Top10 | 100.0 | 185.2 | 142.3 | 140.0 | | |
| 1997 Top10 | 100.0 | 199.1 | 170.9 | 163.3 | | |

And the results? An investor in the 1970s was taking a risk. The results looking forward aren't so great: The portfolio value fell during those turbulent years, while the S&P index rose by nearly one-half. Looking back, holding on to the stocks of the most successful companies (the largest ones at the end of the decade) would have made you some money. In other words, if you could have foreseen the future, you would have done quite well. This is what we expect in normal markets and industries. Neither ordinary people nor even academics have the gift of being able to predict the future.

Looking at the portfolio after 1980, we discovered something quite remarkable: The ability to foresee the future would no longer have given you an edge in terms of the money you would make as an investor in pharmaceutical stocks. The portfolios of the largest firms at the start of the period perform almost exactly as well as those at the end of the period! Essentially, if you had invested at any point in the 1980s or 1990s in any of the top drug companies, you would have realized the same return as if you were able to travel back in time and make your investments based on what you know today. It was easy to predict the future of the biggest pharmaceutical companies since it looked exactly like the recent past. This pattern has lasted for two decades, during which the airwaves and financial pages were full of idle chat about the risks these companies took.

In a nutshell, the risk that large drug companies would have *diverse* fortunes, so evident in the 1970s, disappeared completely after 1980. They *all* do well. No matter how many times industry analysts warn that a patent expiration is going to make this or that company vanish, it hasn't happened—at least in the last quarter-century. And this trend of doing well appears to continue today, although in fairness the evidence suffers a bit because of the short period of measurement. A large part of that stability comes from the fact that the industry has figured out how to price its products so companies stay financially healthy.

If there is little or no doubt about which companies are going to be successful, and the big pharmaceutical companies *always* remain big, profitable (perhaps more than any industry in U.S. history), and growing, an investor certainly doesn't seem to be taking much risk. Perhaps if individual drug candidates could be bought and sold, the pharmaceutical industry's contention that *risk* justifies high prices would resonate. But the largest drug companies can mitigate the risk at the company level by diversifying it according to the *law of large numbers* (that the more times an event occurs, the more predictable the outcome is). They do it just like a fire insurance company. It's the difference between saying that any one house might burn down and saying that the company itself is risky. Investing at the drug company level is a good, solid, and basically *riskless* proposition.

Our findings make the pharmaceutical industry's argument about risk ring hollow. But could this period of exceptional, riskless prosperity be coming to an end? Things look good at the moment, but completely external factors could always rear their ugly head. More to the point, though, industry-specific storm clouds are on the horizon. The blockbuster model described in Chapter 1, "Drugs and Drug Prices," is failing—to be succeeded by a new business model still in progress. A catastrophe may even be waiting in the wings, one linked in part to how the structure of this highly profitable industry has shifted, and also in how science and technology challenge whether that structure—indeed, the current business model of drug discovery and development—makes sense.

> *A catastrophe may even be waiting in the wings, one linked in part to how the structure of this highly profitable industry has shifted, and also in how science and technology challenge whether that structure makes sense.*

## The Shift to Outsourcing

Over these decades of little or no risk, scientific and technological advances, and huge market shifts propelled in part by the profits reaped through DTC advertising, the pharmaceutical industry has evolved into a form and structure that is quite different than what had existed in the earlier part of the twentieth century. Today's panoply includes huge companies that have been around for many decades, new large companies resulting from mergers of major firms, and a host of smaller firms rooted in biotechnology.

Table 4-2 lists the 20 largest U.S. pharmaceutical companies over a 30-year period.

You see quite a bit of durability in the form of familiar names consistently leading the industry: Merck, Pfizer, Bristol-Myers (now Bristol-Myers Squibb), Eli Lilly, Johnson and Johnson, Schering-Plough, and Abbott (now Abbott Laboratories). But many new companies now rival the leaders in size. Most of the changes are due to mergers and acquisitions within the top 20, but there's also the

**TABLE 4-2.** *The Largest Pharmaceutical Companies at Different Dates*

| | Top 20 in the U.S. 1973 | Top 16 in the U.S. 1980 | Top 20 in the U.S. 1997 | Top 20 in the U.S. 2003 |
|---|---|---|---|---|
| 1 | Merck and Co. | Merck and Co. | Merck and Co. | Pfizer |
| 2 | Warner-Lambert | American Home Products | Bristol-Myers Squibb | Merck and Co. |
| 3 | American Home Products | Abbott | American Home Products | Johnson and Johnson |
| 4 | Pfizer | Bristol-Myers | Eli Lilly | Bristol-Myers Squibb |
| 5 | Bristol-Myers | Pfizer | Pfizer | Wyeth |
| 6 | Eli Lilly | Smith Kline | Johnson and Johnson | Eli Lilly |
| 7 | Sterling Drug | Eli Lilly | Abbott | Abbott Laboratories |
| 8 | Squibb | Upjohn | Pharmacia and Upjohn | Amgen |
| 9 | Schering-Plough | Johnson and Johnson | Schering-Plough | Schering-Plough |
| 10 | Upjohn | Schering-Plough | Warner-Lambert | Baxter |
| 11 | Johnson and Johnson | Squibb | Amgen | Genentech |
| 12 | Abbott | Warner-Lambert | Baxter International | Forest Labs |
| 13 | Cyanamid | Sterling Drug | Chiron | Purdue Pharma |
| 14 | Smith Kline | American Cyanamid | Allergan | Allergan |
| 15 | Searle | Searle | Genentech | King |
| 16 | Dow | Dow | ICN Pharmaceuticals | Genzyme |
| 17 | Richardson Merrell | ——— | Genentech | Watson |
| 18 | Robins | ——— | Ivax | Biogen Idec |
| 19 | Morton-Norwich | ——— | Perrigo | Mylan Labs |
| 20 | 3M | ——— | Alpharma | Chiron |

emergence of new science, as the presence of biotechnology companies such as Genentech, Genzyme, and Amgen illustrates.[1]

Mergers among the top pharmaceutical companies have become commonplace. Several factors drive this trend: expectations of excess capacity when patents expire; the search for economies of scale as well as scope, and sometimes for specific assets of the merger partner; even geographic expansion. The largest include Pfizer's $60 billion merger with Pharmacia in 2003 and its $90 billion acquisition of Warner-Lambert in 2000, as well as SmithKline Beecham's $75 billion merger in 2000 with Glaxo Wellcome. The large pharmaceutical companies also acquire smaller firms seeking the financial resources of the big partner.[2]

Smaller firms, which tend to rely on their R & D activities and may not yet have products on the market, also merge. They combine to ensure growth and access to capital, and thus reduce research costs. Mergers between two small companies rarely produce a top-twenty firm, but the evidence suggests that size isn't what guarantees success in the industry. Consider the boom of emerging biotechnology companies. The 1,231 U.S. firms categorized as biotechnology companies in 1992 had climbed to 1,415 by 2005, part of a global industry of 4,203 companies. The new players may enjoy an "attacker's advantage" over the traditional pharmaceutical companies, and the larger players may have to form different subunits or radically reorganize operations to counterattack.[3]

As the large drug companies get bigger, they're also increasingly outsourcing the risk they do incur at what the industry calls the "project level." This includes much of what has traditionally been an in-house activity that is the essence of the modern pharmaceutical industry: drug discovery.

*Drug discovery* is a complex process of identifying promising, beneficial compounds and avoiding problematic ones, and involves selecting therapeutic targets, constructing and managing diverse chemical libraries, and performing early metabolism and toxicity studies. It includes a biological phase and a chemical phase, both of which make use of computers, combinatorial chemistry, and robotic screening.[4]

Until the mid-1990s, drug companies considered all aspects of discovery to be central to development and outsourced only other tasks involved in getting a new drug to market. But it's a lot of work, and as more and more potential drug targets were discovered, and pharmaceutical companies tried to take on more projects, it started to take quite a toll on company resources.[5]

The new millennium has seen the creation of a new drug *discovery* industry, with company growth fueled by the spread of mergers in the broader pharmaceutical industry that displaced so many experienced scientists. And why outsource to these firms? Of every 100,000 compounds screened, only 100 are effective against a target, and only one makes it to the lead compound stage and goes on to become a new drug. Approximately 72 percent of a company's budget for drug development is spent on failed compounds—one of the reasons consistently cited by the industry to explain high prices. Given that it takes 15 years on average for a drug to make it to the market, increasing the efficiency of drug discovery should lead to a huge payoff for the pharmaceutical companies. By contracting out data generation to other companies, for example, pharmaceutical companies can focus on data interpretation and analysis. They can put more effort into understanding what drugs do to your body and what your body does to the drugs, thereby increasing the number of compounds ready for clinical research.[6]

## Big Money Involved in Outsourcing

One of the first aspects of drug discovery that was outsourced was the chemistry involved in developing a new drug. The market for outsourced discovery is huge—an estimated $4.1 billion in 2005 and predicted to grow to $7.2 billion by 2009.[7]

*Lead optimization*—the process of determining whether a compound found to be effective against the target can be converted into a drug candidate for testing—is also a major arena for outsourcing. The process involves synthetic and medicinal chemistry, biochemical and functional screening, computer-aided drug design, and pharmacological studies. Today, many companies spread across the globe specialize in lead optimization, and by 2004 most pharmaceutical companies were outsourcing at least some lead optimization. The market was worth $1.63 billion in 2003, and is expected to increase to $3.53 billion in 2007. With such a booming industry, it is no surprise that many drug discovery companies are incorporating lead optimization services into their repertoire.[8] Meanwhile, older companies that were already conducting lead optimization look to offer a greater range of services— even proprietary drug discovery research.[9]

Increasingly, companies—even the largest firms—are contracting out the essence of drug discovery itself to companies around the world.[10] Indian, Chinese, and Russian drug discovery companies are growing, and are striking more and more long-term deals with Western pharmaceutical firms. Five major pharmaceutical companies—Pfizer, Eli Lilly, Merck and Co., Novartis, and Bristol-Myers Squibb—account for 25 percent of all drug discovery outsourcing. As companies grow more accustomed to contracting out drug discovery and the external companies become more familiar with new technologies, the industry expects to see an improvement in the quality of lead compounds and a decrease in costs and development time.[11]

Science isn't the only reason for outsourcing. Drug companies save money, too—especially when they outsource to companies in the developing world. Employing a chemist working on drug discovery in the United States costs roughly $250,000 per year. Hiring a chemist in India, doing the same work, costs only $65,000 to $70,000 per year. One estimate puts the cost in China at $45,000 to $70,000 per year.[12]

## Outsourcing Clinical Trials

In addition to drug discovery, another key part of the development process has also become a huge outsourced component of the overall pharmaceutical sector: testing.

Testing a drug before it can reach the market is a lengthy process that requires a massive amount of resources and often becomes

*Since the 1990s, out-sourced clinical research has become an extremely lucrative business.*

a bottleneck that many drug companies prefer to let external firms manage. Since the 1990s, outsourced clinical research has become an extremely lucrative business and a huge number of *Contract Research Organizations (CROs)* have emerged. These firms can save drug firms vast sums of money by working on a per-product basis: They do their job and go away, and the pharmaceutical company doesn't have to pay for people to sit around waiting for the next product to reach the clinical testing phase.

How lucrative is the CRO business? Stacy Martin and Patricia Daly were nurses working in the management of Pfizer's clinical trials, but left to take advantage of their employer's increasing use of outside firms to conduct many aspects of clinical trials. The new company they founded in 1995, Metropolitan Research Associates (MRA), had grown by 2004 to 120 employees and $12 million in revenues.[13]

MRA is a comprehensive CRO, one of several large firms that works with multiple pharmaceutical companies at once and handles all parts of clinical trials, including studies that continue after drug approval. Other, smaller firms work on a per-project basis and specialize in only certain aspects of the trial process. And in the past decade, pharmaceutical companies have had the option of outsourcing to CROs outside of the United States.

"Offshoring" clinical trials to India, China, Latin America, or Eastern Europe offers a lot of advantages to the pharmaceutical industry. One is the cost—clinical trials in India, for example, cost 40 percent less than they would in the United States,[14] and sometimes the savings are even greater. Another benefit is the efficiency with which these foreign firms can recruit patients. Recruiting test subjects in India or China generally takes half the time required in the

United States.[15] In India, with its 3 million cancer patients, 10 million psychiatric patients, 25 million diabetics, 30 million heart patients, and 5 million HIV-positive citizens, participating in clinical trials is the only way many people can get treatment.[16] SIRO Clinpharm, a CRO based in India, was able to recruit 750 patients for German drug manufacturer Mucos Pharma within 18 months,[17] whereas in Europe it took double that time to find a mere 100 volunteers.

Some 90 percent of SIRO's business comes from international clients, and the business has grown 60 to 80 percent each year since the firm's founding in 1997.[18] In fact, CROs based in India saw their revenues from foreign outsourcing rise from $30 million in 2001 to $122 million in 2003.[19] In May 2005, approximately 10,000 people in India were taking part in more than 100 clinical trials.[20]

## *What about Manufacturing?*

One aspect of the structure of the pharmaceutical industry that rarely gets discussed is manufacturing. Economists and others often dismiss pharmaceutical manufacturing costs as trivial compared to those for R & D and marketing. This view is fueled by remarks like that made by one pharmaceutical executive, who stated that it costs about "a penny a pill" to produce his company's blockbuster antihistamine. But the manufacturing process is actually more complex, highly regulated, and more costly than most people realize. An examination of the annual reports of the large pharmaceutical firms reveals that the proportion of revenues devoted to manufacturing (*cost of goods sold*) is typically in the neighborhood of 25 percent, and sometimes as high as 35 percent.

Why so much? When a drug firm decides to mount its initial human trials on a new drug, it must produce a limited number of doses to be administered in the studies. First, though, there needs to be a manufacturing process developed to meet those early needs. Then, if the trial results are favorable, production needs to be scaled up to meet the likely demands of the marketplace. Firms must comply with FDA regulatory requirements: adhere to "Good Manufacturing Practices;" maintain detailed records; and submit to plant inspections. All of this comes at a cost. (Not to mention the additional costs that result from failure to comply. Many firms have, in recent years, been cited by FDA inspectors for not meeting certain requirements. Some have been fined and some have restructured their manufacturing operations—resulting in manufacturing costs that account for a particularly high proportion of revenues in some years.)

Even if the raw material costs for chemical (often called *small molecule*) drugs are as low as the executive described, the planning and compliance costs are not. And while raw material costs for *biological drugs* (vaccines, proteins, antibodies) may be even lower than for chemical drugs, processing costs can be much greater. Add to this that the FDA considers that "the manufacturing process defines the product" for nearly all biological products, and you can see how the resources required to satisfy the regulatory agency can be quite significant.

*Generic pharmaceutical firms*, which don't typically discover and develop drugs but only manufacture and sell them after patents expire, are subject to the same FDA regulations. Because they often price their products at 10 to 25 percent of the price of the brand-name product, it's a safe bet that they must manufacture the drugs quite inexpensively and efficiently. After all, their business is low-margin. Generic drug firms, in fact, may well represent the future of pharmaceutical manufacturing.

## Lots More Could be Improved

Even with the advantages of outsourcing clinical research and the potential for more cost-efficient manufacturing, and despite all the advances in biopharmaceutical knowledge, companies looking to get new drugs on the market continue to face challenges. Current methods for compound synthesis, storage, and retrieval need improvement. Target selection and validation must be more accurate. A greater emphasis must be placed on acquiring good data related to a number of technical criteria including adsorption, distribution, metabolism, excretion, and toxicity—what pharmaceutical scientists call ADMET—early in the discovery process. And then there is the issue of clinical trials. They comprise some 80 percent of the cost of drug development—an investment no company wants to make until there's some assurance that the drug being tested isn't toxic. All of this unfolds over a *very* long period. It takes about 13 years in total to move a candidate drug through the full discovery and development process, and then there's the wait for FDA approval. At the end of the 1980s, FDA approval took between two and three years, but since then the FDA introduced a fast-track approval process for so-called *priority drugs*—anything considered to have potentially exceptional value to public health. Today, a priority drug typically takes only six months or so to be approved. The good news is that rather than increasing the approval time for all other drugs, that too has decreased—albeit nowhere near as much.[21]

*It takes about 13 years in total to move a candidate drug through the full discovery and development process, and then there's the wait for FDA approval.*

## THE PROMISE OF SYSTEMS BIOLOGY

Drug discovery has always been a *reductionist process*, focusing on small details such as the interaction between compounds before moving into *in vitro* models and clinical trials. And it's not until clinical trials that scientists realize the shortcomings of a compound that had a desired reaction in the lab. This is one of the main reasons the number of NDAs approved remains low, despite the high number of INDs.

*Systems biology*, which focuses on the big picture, offers a possible solution. Researchers combine data about genes, proteins, and metabolites to generate a comprehensive picture of the connections between the different parts. They collect information about entire biological systems and use computer models, simulations, and even robotic models to identify the pathways involved in a particular disease or determine whether a drug is acting on the intended pathway. Systems biology's proponents expect it to be very effective in finding ADMET data. Since the process starts at the systems or clinical level rather than at the molecular level, scientists know quickly whether a compound will have a harmful impact on the subject. Systems biology promises other breakthroughs in drug discovery, too. For instance, it's difficult to predict through typical drug-discovery methods whether combination products involving a number of drugs administered together will achieve a desired effect. Systems biology, though, *begins* with achieving the desired effect—making discovering these therapies much more likely.[22]

It will be a while before systems biology's full impact is apparent, but as technology improves and advances are made in the field, this new approach to drug discovery may well shorten the drug-discovery process and make it more cost-effective.[23]

If anything, the picture of the pharmaceutical industry reveals challenges and complexities. Looking forward, we see opposing tendencies. On the one hand, scientific advances, directed searching, and lead optimization all suggest that drug companies will continue to prosper and grow, which in turn suggests that the innovations will keep coming. On the other hand, drug prices are beyond many people's capacity to pay, they aren't falling, and innovation promises to push prices even higher. Meanwhile, the decline in the number of NMEs and the emphasis on niche drugs has provoked a contest between drug companies that want to charge ever-higher prices and insurers that feel they cannot afford to offer these drugs to their subscribers.

Private insurers can, of course, pass on the increased costs to consumers—but how much longer will that work? Government itself is a major health insurer, and with the new Medicare drug benefit (Part D), it's gotten even bigger. How can the government afford to pay these high prices?

We're at a crucial juncture. Could skyrocketing drug prices, justified in the name of innovation and risk, actually make the technological advances come crumbling down around us? That remains to be seen, although the dark clouds are appearing. One thing is for certain, though: The most recent effort by the government to ensure access to needed medicines is no way to lower drug prices. That is the subject of Chapter 5, "How *Not* to Lower Drug Prices."

## *Endnotes*

[1] Sellers, L. J. 2004. Special report: PharmExec 50. *Pharmaceutical Executive* 24:5, 60.

[2] Merger size measured by both nominal and real value. Research indicates a high rate of M&A activity in the 1980s and 1990s. See: Danzon, P. M. et al. 2004. Mergers and acquisitions in the pharmaceutical and biotech industries. Philadelphia: The Wharton School—University of Pennsylvania. http://hc.wharton.upenn.edu/danzon/html/recent_working_papers.htm (accessed April 21, 2007).

[3] Biotechnology Industry Organization. 2005. Number of biotech companies, 1992–2001. www.bio.org/ataglance/bio/200210num.asp (accessed April 21, 2007). See also: Ernst and Young. 2006. Ernst and Young's beyond borders: A global perspective. *Biotech Industry Overview and 2005 Year in Review*. www.ey.com/beyondborders (accessed April 21, 2007). See also: Pisano, G. P. 2000. Transforming economics of the biopharmaceuticals industry. Presentation at BIO 2000 Economic Forum (March 27). www.thebiotechclub.org/industry/articles/transforming_econ.php (accessed April 21, 2007).

[4] One company, Abbott Laboratories, developed three times as many compounds for clinical research in 2004 as it did five years earlier thanks to computational chemistry. See: Klopack, T. G. 2004. Today's drug discovery. *R & D Directions* 10:2.

[5] According to Michael Trova, senior vice president at AMRI (one of the leading providers of drug discovery services), the first example of discovery outsourcing occurred in 1995. See: Boswell, C. 2005. Discovery outsourcing increases. *Chemical Market Reporter* 267:14, 14.

[6] Clark, D. E. and Newton, C. G. 2004. Outsourcing lead optimization: The quiet revolution. *Drug Discovery Today* 9:11; Klopack, 2004, *op. cit.*

[7] PRLeap. 2006. Drug discovery outsourcing market set to exceed $7 billion by 2009. March 6. www.prleap.com/pr/28329/ (accessed April 21, 2007).

[8] For instance, Albany Molecular Research, one of the earliest (founded in 1991), has 850 employees in New York, Chicago, and Seattle, and does medicinal chemistry, combinatorial chemistry, computational chemistry, and physical chemistry, among other things. Aurigene Discovery Technologies, founded in 2001, has 60 scientists. Although the company is based in Boston, it also has research facilities in Bangalore, India. WuXi PharmaTech is a company of 190 scientists based in Shanghai, China, and specializing in library design, medicinal chemistry, lead optimization, radiochemistry, and a wide range of other functions. See: Clark and Newton, 2004, *op. cit.*

[9] Cush, S. and D. Tapolczay. 2000. Companies look to outsource chemistry. *Drug Discovery and Development*, May. Klopack, 2004, *op. cit.*

[10] As with other phases of pharmaceutical research and development, drug discovery is increasingly being contracted to foreign companies. Indian, Chinese, and Russian drug discovery companies are growing, and are striking more and more long-term deals with Western drug companies; Shasun Chemicals and Drugs, a company based in Chennai, India, expanded a two-year-old relationship with Eli Lilly in 2003, giving the company research rights to three of Lilly's drugs in development. WuXi PharmaTech, mentioned above, began a research collaboration with Merck in 2003 to design lead generation libraries and intermediates. See: McCoy, M. and J-F. Tremblay. 2003. Tapping foreign brains for profit. *Chemical and Engineering News* 81:48, 15–23.

[11] Still, U.S. drug discovery companies claim an advantage in sophisticated drug discovery chemistry. Thomas D'Ambra, chairman and CEO of Albany Molecular Research (AMR), one of the leading firms in the industry, believes processes such as lead optimization and structure-activity relationship studies will stay within the United States. Aside from the more advanced technology available here, D'Ambra believes that U.S. drug firms will not trust foreign firms with the protection of intellectual property. A new molecule or compound becomes a firm's intellectual property once it shows a desired effect against a drug target. Then the developer becomes very protective. Yet despite D'Ambra's claims, growth among Western drug-discovery firms has begun to slow, and AMR itself reported declining revenues from contract research, with an 18 percent drop from 2002 to 2003. See: Clark and Newton, 2004, op. cit.

[12] According to Mukund Chorghade, president of the pharmaceutical sciences division at D and O Pharmachem. Many offshore discovery companies are also trying to build their infrastructure to include more sophisticated research capabilities. Chorghade says his company can even provide structure-activity relationship studies, one of the more complex processes of drug discovery. Aurigene, another Indian

firm, hired veterinarians to care for animals used for *in vivo* pharmokinetics studies and toxicology work, another sophisticated phase of the discovery process. McCoy, M. 2003. Tapping foreign brains for profit. *Chemical and Engineering News* 81:48, 15–23.

[13] Boss-Bicak, S. 2004. Clinical trial firms prove efficacy. *Crain's New York Business* 20:43.

[14] Sinha, G. 2004. Outsourcing drug work. *Scientific American* 291:2.

[15] Rai, S. 2004. Drug companies cut costs with foreign clinical trials. *New York Times,* February 24:C4.

[16] DeWet, M. 2005. Drug companies mull ethics of using India for clinical trials. *Business Customwire*, May 2.

[17] Sinha, 2004, *op. cit.*

[18] *Ibid.*

[19] Rai, 2004, *op. cit.*

[20] DeWet, 2005, *op. cit.*

[21] DiLorenzo, 2005, *op. cit.* See also: Saftlas, H. and W. Diller. 2005. Health care: Pharmaceuticals. *Standard and Poor's Industry Surveys*, July 21.

[22] For example, Gene Network Sciences mapped a human cancer cell, including 500 genes, proteins, and their interactions. Scientists used the model to show that if a so-called important protein is targeted and removed, others can take its place. Now the company is trying to redirect research to find a target set of proteins that may result in a much higher chance of destroying the cell. See: Henry, C. M. 2005. Systems biology. *Chemical and Engineering News* 83:7, 47–55.

[23] *Ibid.*

# CHAPTER FIVE

## HOW *NOT* TO LOWER DRUG PRICES

*Insurance: An ingenious modern game of chance in which
the player is permitted to enjoy the comfortable conviction
that he is beating the man who keeps the table.*

—Ambrose Bierce

If there's any lingering skepticism that drug prices are high, often so high that they limit access for those who need medicine, a look back at a phenomenon that began in the mid-1990s ought to dispel any doubt. Remember senior citizens traveling to Canada by the busload to buy prescription drugs? The story eventually forced the government to take action. But what followed is a lesson in how *not* to lower drug prices.

The rumblings began in Minnesota in 1994, where a small group of citizens decided something had to be done about their lack of access to drugs at prices they could afford. They established a statewide network of pharmacists willing to import prescription drugs from Mexico, where the prices charged were considerably lower. But the FDA got wind of it, alleged it was illegal, and the scheme collapsed.[1]

Over the next two years, their focus shifted to Canada—and *direct* action. A growing number of senior citizens in Minnesota took bus trips into Canada to buy brand-name drugs at much lower prices. A Minnesota Senior Federation sponsored a trip to Winnipeg and turned it into a protest highlighting that the seniors spent

58 cents in Canada to purchase what cost a dollar in the United States. In response, U.S. drug firms argued that the "price controls in countries such as Canada" might make the trip attractive for seniors, but "force U.S. consumers to pay more for research and development." That didn't kill the story, though; by the end of the 1990s, it seemed as if you couldn't turn on the TV news without watching another busload of seniors crossing the border. Senior citizens felt compelled to make the trip because the U.S. system ate deeply into their retirement funds to pay for medicines they desperately needed.[2]

Even as the FDA stepped in, asserting that seniors were importing "unapproved" drugs, the bus trip phenomenon could not be stopped. And since seniors account for a significant voting bloc, it's no surprise that the politicians took notice. President Clinton ordered a study of prescription drug prices in October 1999, declaring, "No senior should have to forego or cut back on lifesaving medicine because of the cost. Neither should any senior be forced to get on the bus to Canada where the same medicines cost so much less." He recommended a government-funded overhaul of Medicare that would have expanded the system to include drug benefits, using the government's strong bargaining power to lower drug prices. The pharmaceutical industry, concerned that price controls might follow, lobbied Congress to take a different approach: expand Medicare by subsidizing private insurance companies and Health Maintenance Organizations (HMOs) to cover drug costs. When the 2000 presidential campaign began, a debate over reforming Medicare to include some sort of prescription drug benefit to ease the seniors' burden began in earnest, with the drug companies using their clout with elected officials to influence the outcome.[3]

The pharmaceutical industry's public salvo came in March 2000. TV and radio ads aimed at deterring seniors from crossing the border into Canada to make their purchases claimed that buying drugs in another country puts innovation at risk. As pressure mounted on government representatives to do something, the industry argued for the need to fund research and development and touted the superiority of the U.S. hospital and medical system. But things were getting beyond the control of the powerful drug lobby. The Maine legislature even passed a bill in May 2000 that created price limits—something virtually unheard of in the United States—if the pharmaceutical industry did not lower drug prices in that state. "[M]ore than a dozen lobbyists showed up at the first hearing on the state's proposed prescription drug law—some descending on Augusta in three corporate jets." Other Northeastern states considered taking similar action. By the summer of 2000, Congress had passed bills relaxing importation laws on prescription drugs, but they were never implemented because of safety concerns raised by the U.S. Department of Health and Human Services. It didn't matter, though, because seniors continued to "break the law," using any way they could to get their prescription drugs.[4]

The pharmaceutical industry decided to up the ante and target the new law in Maine directly. SmithKline Beecham, defiantly refusing to alter its prices in Maine, changed its supply routes and shipped drugs to wholesalers in neighboring states. A week later, a coalition of drug producers filed a lawsuit against the state of Maine, charging that its new law was unconstitutional. But none of these steps undid what mattered most to the industry: By July 2004, drug purchases from Canada had reached the $1 billion mark.[5]

This was the backdrop to the federal government finally taking action. The government, though, did not go after the high prices that were at the root of the problem. Instead, a reform of Medicare that had been languishing in Congress for years suddenly made it to the front burner. It even won the support of the American Association of Retired Persons (AARP), obviously—and controversially—desperate for something, *anything*, to be done for its members. A new bill was narrowly passed into law in 2003 that added a prescription drug benefit to the program—the *Medicare Prescription Drug, Improvement, and Modernization Act (MMA)*. The new benefit is typically referred to as *Medicare Part D*.

This new law is fatally flawed because it tries to solve the crisis of access to medicines *and* preserve the financial resources of the pharmaceutical companies that are used to fund research and development without fixing the skewed incentives that drive drug discovery and development. It's an impossible balancing act. Billions of dollars are at stake, though, so it's no wonder that the fingers of the private, profit-driven pharmaceutical industry itself can be found all over the legislation that brought Medicare Part D to life.

> *The Medicare Part D law is fatally flawed because it tries to solve the crisis of access to medicines and preserve the financial resources of the pharmaceutical companies that are used to fund R & D without fixing the skewed incentives that drive drug discovery and development. It's an impossible balancing act.*

The law's crafters sought a way to improve access by lowering out-of-pocket costs for those most in need of medications *without* addressing the prices drug companies charge. The law even forbids Medicare from negotiating with drug companies for lower prices. That means someone has to pay the difference. That someone is you, either in your role as taxpayer or as a direct "beneficiary" of the new plan.

The original estimate of a $400 billion cost to the government over 10 years was key to the bill's passage, and it was sold to Congress partly on the argument that it would cost no more. But before the bill was passed, members of the Bush administration realized that even this huge figure was wishful thinking. As administration spokespersons stood firmly behind the $400 billion figure in public, the president's men were working hard to keep the real numbers secret. Richard Foster, chief actuary for Medicare, said that he knew six months before the

MMA passed Congress that the cost could be $600 billion. He said that the program administrator, Thomas Scully, repeatedly threatened to fire him if he told Congress the real projections. Scully, who had run Medicare and Medicaid for more than two years, announced within a month after Medicare Part D was signed into law that he had been given a waiver to look for a private-sector job while working to win passage of the new law and would be leaving government to join an Atlanta law firm that represents drug companies and other private healthcare providers—validating the view that the new law was crafted with a lot of help from the pharmaceutical industry.[6]

Whether it's $400 billion or $600 billion or the $724 billion over ten years claimed by actuaries in February 2006, how could a bill cost so much and do absolutely nothing to reduce prices? The answer lies in how privatization theory has been applied to medical care.[7]

## *"Managed Competition" in Health Care*

Medicare Part D went into effect on January 1, 2006, with two purposes: extend federal prescription drug insurance to senior citizens on Medicare (omitted since the program's creation in the 1960s) and reduce the growth rate of Medicare costs. The idea behind the law is to shift part of Medicare coverage from the government to private insurers to induce competition in the hope that this will solve the problem of growing costs. In the healthcare world, this concept is known as *managed competition*.

The idea of managed competition goes back to two 1978 articles by economist Alain Enthoven published in the *New England Journal of Medicine*. He proposed a new type of health plan, based on the belief that what he called "perverse incentives" are the main driver of cost increases, and that these are an inherent part of how health care is financed. Enthoven wanted to replace the traditional model of paying doctors and hospitals for specific services with something very different. You know it today as your HMO.[8]

Enthoven did not discuss drugs in his articles, but we can rephrase his bold assertion about "perverse incentives" in the context of prescription pharmaceuticals. Why do Americans spend more on prescription drugs than a generation ago? Drugs do so much more for us, so we buy more. People with drug coverage as part of their health insurance may well buy even more drugs because they don't pay the retail cost. As Enthoven might put it, the low cost of drugs to these people is a *perverse incentive* that leads to increased spending. Economists call this a *moral hazard*, meaning the effect of actions that help some individuals but hurt others, because those taking the action do not bear all the costs of what they do. For instance, doctor visits are inexpensive for you if you have health insurance, so you will likely use medical services without considering cost. That ends up driving up the costs for everyone else. Hence, in essence, this exemplifies Enthoven's "perverse incentive."

Every beginning economics textbook asserts that prices should reflect the cost of producing something efficiently, but insurance does not fit this model. With almost all insurance, consumers become subject to a moral hazard, accepting too much risk because they are insured against expenses that accrue when they lose a gamble. For example, if you're insured and your house burns down or you're in a traffic accident, then your paying the full cost of replacing your home or vehicle is unlikely. To minimize risks, we accept pervasive moral hazard from the smallest individual actions to the international economic relations among countries—consider bailout loans, for instance. Enthoven argued that the primary perverse incentive in medical care as a whole came from the very *presence* of health insurance, especially the type of coverage that provides benefits without any deductible. This shielded consumers from most out-of-pocket healthcare costs and thereby distorted their view of the cost of health care—if they even thought about the cost at all.[9]

Enthoven's solution: Reform the healthcare system by introducing managed competition to remove these incentives. Since prices embody the distorted incentives, this would mean—in practice—that drug companies would charge *higher* prices to consumers. And while managed competition would raise the marginal cost of medical care for consumers, it would reduce the marginal return to health-care insurers and providers. Enthoven theorized that this would lead the very consumers who care so little about saving money on what seemed like "free" medical care to reconsider things, look at the costs, and ultimately reduce their purchases. Doctors and hospitals would be paid less for procedures, and because they would earn less they would lose the incentive to do things like order extra—and costly—tests. This, in turn, would eliminate the perverse incentive for producers—doctors, hospitals, and drug companies—who are paid on a fee-for-service basis to sell as many services as they could. That's the basic idea behind your HMO.

"Letting the market rule" is not completely unfettered, however. Managed competition, as Enthoven conceived it, does involve some regulation. So-called *sponsor organizations* establish rules of equity, select participating plans, manage the enrollment process, create price-elastic demand (that is, sensitivity to price changes), manage risk selection, and ensure that every health-insurance policy satisfies some minimum quality standards. In this way, the sponsor avoids a "race to the bottom" in which healthcare carriers offer progressively lower prices but with reduced coverage quality as well. The sponsor creates a level playing field on which the different healthcare carriers compete for consumer favor.

## THREE KEY ELEMENTS TO THE THEORY OF MANAGED COMPETITION

The theory of managed competition in health care has three key elements.

1. First, consumers must be given a choice of health plans, with financial incentives and information to make appropriate choices.

> That choice functions best when many health insurers compete aggressively to enroll plan participants.[10]
>
> 2. Second, employers must provide their employees the same fixed subsidy for all plans. If consumers want to purchase health care from a carrier that offers more comprehensive coverage, they should pay the full cost of this added insurance. Only then will consumers choose the appropriate level of health insurance based on its cost.
>
> 3. Third, but equally important, the healthcare delivery system must be integrated with the healthcare financing system. Doctors shouldn't be individual professionals operating on a fee-for-service basis, but employees or contractors of cooperative health plans subject to external financial constraints that promote economic efficiency by attempting to lower their costs and outbid their competitors for business. That's the idea behind HMOs in which doctors are paid by *capitation*, that is, they are paid a fixed amount for each patient regardless of how many services or the nature of services they provide. Only then, the theory argues, will providers benefit financially by *reducing* rather than increasing medical services.

What, then, is wrong with managed competition? To begin with, most consumers don't like it. It's no accident that books and movies routinely depict HMOs as unfeeling and even malevolent. Healthcare providers don't like it, either; it makes them feel like grocers, not professionals. Doctors deal with conditions fraught with uncertainty that require professional judgment, and—as Nobel Laureate economist Kenneth Arrow said four decades ago—consumers cannot understand the complexities of modern medicine, particularly when distracted by illness, and the market, even guided by the choices of informed consumers, cannot possibly police suppliers of medical services. Arrow's view is borne out in the effects created by TV advertisements for prescription drugs, which stimulate consumers to second-guess their doctors based on very little information.[11]

Large industrial firms, too, have been skeptical of managed competition. They were supposed to act as the sponsors, but they don't trust their workers to act as informed medical consumers or trust the market to offer the right choices. Instead, most companies purchase health coverage as they would other inputs to their production processes. And while large companies have incorporated modest financial incentives into this industrial approach to purchasing, a survey of the *Fortune 500* conducted by one of the authors showed that the theory of managed competition is followed mostly in name only. The largest companies sampled the recommendations of managed competition, adopting one or another of the three elements of this theory. However, as explained earlier, all three elements are necessary if managed competition is to provide its presumed benefits.[12]

Two decades of managed competition haven't reduced overall healthcare costs. While there was a brief respite from these high costs starting in 1993, and many people thought managed competition had done the trick, medical costs resumed their dramatic rise

> *Two decades of managed competition haven't reduced overall healthcare costs.*

by 1999.[13] Meanwhile, health-insurance companies, hospitals, and physicians all underwent tremendous changes with the introduction of Enthoven's ideas to the U.S. healthcare system—but not drug companies. They were not included among the healthcare providers that had to alter how they do business under managed competition. Medicare Part D hasn't changed that; the disciples of managed competition decided to allow drug companies to continue doing business as usual.

## Medicare Part D and Privatization

Nevertheless, it was in the *spirit* of managed competition that the government adopted Medicare Part D in 2003. The Bush administration, advocating the bill's passage, reiterated again and again the importance of giving people a *choice* of drug plans, and offered the Federal Employees Health Benefit Plan as a model, since it provides the same reimbursement for any plan—meaning that more expensive plans cost federal employees more. The bill that was passed into law incorporated choice and uniform subsidies among plans, two of managed care's three key elements. Left out, though, was the third element: integrating the drug component of healthcare delivery with overall healthcare financing.[14]

Doctors have been forced into HMOs and specialty groups that take financial risks they previously did not experience, and they are neither as happy nor as wealthy as they once were. The drug companies, by contrast, still charge the equivalent of fee-for-service, earning more when people are sick. For Medicare Part D to have included managed competition's third component, it would have meant that the drug companies had to do business more like doctors now do, with their financial success linked to measurable improvements in people's health. Even with this so-called *pay for performance* initiative, Medicare does nothing to change the situation.

With Medicare Part D, people choose voluntarily among private plans. This is the key element of the new program: It privatizes an important part of Medicare. But the way these private plans work isn't left completely to market forces; the law states explicitly what they can and cannot do. And rather than having "sponsors" as Enthoven conceived them, the law has the effect of reducing and directing the choices of individuals, much the way large corporations are doing for healthcare in general.

Further, the government subsidizes the insurance companies offering drug benefits under Medicare Part D so the price can be low enough to make these new plans more attractive than other options available on the open market. So, privatization is why the drug benefit costs taxpayers so much—and why the cost is rising.

The "basic" Medicare Part D benefit costs a person, on average, $35 per month for prescriptions. First you pay a $250 deductible (expected to increase over time with inflation) before the Medicare insurance kicks in. Consumers then pay 25 percent of the price of the drug at the pharmacy or wherever they get their prescriptions filled, up to the initial coverage limit of $2,250. Then there is a gap in coverage until a consumer's spending for prescription drugs reaches $3,600, corresponding to about $5,100 in total drug spending per year. Plan members are responsible for paying the full cost for their prescriptions in the coverage gap between $2,250 and $5,100. Medicare pays 95 percent of prescription drug costs in excess of $5,100.

Press reports have indicated growing anger among senior citizens who have hit the gap, which is called the *doughnut hole*. Many say they didn't understand how the law worked. Others are outraged that they must continue to pay their premiums despite receiving no benefits during the gap in coverage.[15]

The doughnut hole idea was created after attempts were made to lower the cost of medical care with so-called *catastrophic insurance*— extensive coverage that kicks in, for example, if you become ill or have an accident that requires massive medical intervention. Economists love this kind of insurance, which works well for automobiles and homes.[16] In the healthcare world, though, the catastrophe model has proven unpopular, so a related type of consumer-driven health plan was created that provides benefits for smaller, more routine medical expenses. To make such a package affordable, the plan provides only limited payments up front and includes a large deductible for the disaster component. In between, in the doughnut hole, consumers pay the full cost of the drugs they use.

The reality is that the doughnut hole in Medicare Part D forces consumers to pay more and shifts costs to end users. Let's look at an example. First, the law is based on an assumption that people are "average." The average elderly person spent about $2,000 a year for prescription drugs before 2006. To better illustrate the plan, we'll calculate the cost to consumers at $2,250. The program pays $1,500 of this, that is, three-quarters of the spending over the $250 deductible. The cost of the premium is $420—that is, $35 per month for 12 months. The deductible is $250. The proportion of drug costs paid by the consumer after the deductible has been exhausted is $500. So, the total cost to the consumer is $420 + $250 + $500 = $1,170. The consumer gets $2,250 worth of drugs, and pays only about 50 percent of this total cost, but only those drugs on the formulary of his or her insurer are available for purchase. The companies offering this plan can choose which drugs to include in their plans, subject to guidelines explained below.

Very few elderly people are average, however. Those lucky enough to be below the average gain nothing from this drug program until they've shelled out more than $800 for prescription drugs in a year, since they have to pay the monthly premiums and the annual deductible before the insurance even kicks in. If they spend $1,000, they gain a little, paying $858 (including the monthly premium) for this quantity of medicine and saving less than 15 percent of their drug costs. Those unlucky enough to spend $5,000 a year on medicines pay $420 + $250 + $500 + $2,750 = $3,920. (The added $2,750 is for the prescription drugs they had to purchase in the doughnut gap, when Medicare Part D does not pay.) These consumers get about a 20 percent cost reduction for their medicine.

Frances Blue, a retired teacher with lung cancer, found herself trapped immediately in the doughnut hole. She was unable to afford her Part D co-payments to get her cancer-treating drugs, and her income from pension and Social Security disability payments was barely too high to qualify her for charitable assistance. "Now, as her cancer spreads slowly through her lungs, Ms. Blue is getting no medicine at all. 'I've had a month of crying.'"[17]

Medicare Part D's basic design ends up helping, in essence, only sick people who have enough income to spend $4,000 on prescription drugs. The horror stories for those who cannot afford the $4,000 "entry fee" are rampant. Does this sound like a way to solve the problem of access to needed medications for the elderly? Does this sound like an effective way to reduce drug prices?[18]

> *Medicare Part D's basic design ends up helping, in essence, only sick people who have enough income to spend $4,000 on prescription drugs.*

## The "Untouchable" Pharmaceutical Industry

A completely cynical view of Medicare Part D might be that the reform was crafted *only* to create the *illusion* of solving the problem of access to drugs, letting the government off the hook on a huge part of the cost while ensuring that the drug makers and private health plans did as well as ever financially. That Congress and the president prohibited the government from bargaining with drug companies to lower prices only buttresses this view—reinforced again in April 2007 when Senate Republicans blocked the Democratic majority's efforts to allow Medicare to negotiate lower prices.[19] A more nuanced, realistic view focuses on the limitations inherent in the effort to solve the access problem while ensuring future innovation and economic health in the context of the existing system. We maintain that as things stand today, you can address one only at the expense of the other, but not both concurrently—unless you adopt a new approach.

The new law's main failure may be that it does nothing to change the fundamental ways in which the pharmaceutical industry conducts its business and is organized—which, as explained in earlier chapters, both contribute to the high prices of prescription drugs. Instead, the law attempts to make consumers react to certain incentives. For instance, the law specifically gives the private health plans the tools to manage patients' access to medicines and keep a lid on how much they access the plans. The plans do this by negotiating discounts from drug firms and by keeping their enrollees' use of drugs, especially the higher-priced ones, in check—just like PBMs. The main mechanism for achieving this is the drug *formulary*—a list of medicines to which elderly plan members can gain relatively easy access. Rather than offering essentially unlimited access to any FDA-approved drug, the plans use drug formularies to restrict choice. (Ironically, formularies were originally conceived as the list of drugs either available or needed to address all the ills of the population.) In addition, plans implement a variety of so-called *benefit management tools*—in essence, hassles and/or penalties—to guide patients towards older drugs (available as generics) or those for which the plan has negotiated a large discount.

How does all this play out if you belong to a health plan? Here's a typical scenario. Fill a prescription for a drug available as a generic, and you pay the lowest co-payment rate, say, $10 for a month's supply. Perhaps you pay $25 for the next tier of "preferred" drugs, usually branded medicines for which the health plan negotiated good discounts. For $40, you can fill a prescription for drugs in the next-highest tier; perhaps you saw a TV ad or read about them on the Internet. That leaves other drugs, probably with very high prices, that can be accessed only through an "exceptions" or "appeals" process—meaning a lot of paperwork for doctor and patient, time delays, and possible penalties resulting in higher costs. These kinds of management tools, superimposed on formularies, have existed for more than a decade. Most research shows that these approaches make patients' access to needed medicines much more difficult, and do little or nothing to lower total healthcare costs.[20]

The flexibility Medicare Part D offers the health plans to settle on different mixes of easily accessed drugs is also the key to how insurers' drug plans are aided in their negotiations for discounts from the drug companies. The greatest discounts come not from high-volume purchases, but rather when a drug plan moves market share from one drug-company competitor to another—as discussed earlier with PBMs. This gives drug companies another way to make money besides selling the most drugs possible. Here you see clearly the hand of the pharmaceutical industry lobbyists in crafting the law.

The underlying idea is that drug companies will compete for their products to become "preferred" members of a plan's formulary—presumably with lower enrollee co-payments than for competing therapeutic substitutes. You can see this with the stomach acid–reducing class of drugs that includes Nexium, Prevacid, and Protonix. When a health plan opted to attach a $25 co-payment to a month's supply of one of these drugs and a $40 co-payment to the others, it received a large discount from the maker of the first drug in exchange for moving an expected proportion of patients to this preferred drug.

How were these formularies established? Fortunately, Congress did take some action in constructing the law to protect the elderly from plans that might choose to put their own financial health ahead of its patients' well being. Under Medicare Part D, the plans cannot "select" their covered populations by leaving certain drugs off their formularies that are needed by people whose chronic conditions would make them high utilizers of expensive medicines. Instead, the bill mandated the development of a *model formulary* that the government can use as a yardstick to gauge compliance with the law's intent. Charged with developing the model formulary was the *United States Pharmacopeia (USP)*, an independent, nonprofit, non-political organization founded in 1820 that has played an historic role in setting purity standards for chemicals used in drug manufacturing and has, over the years, served other public-interest roles. But even in that process you see the tremendous political influence not only of the pharmaceutical industry but also of the insurers.

USP created an expert panel called the *Model Guidelines Expert Committee (MGEC)*, comprising 18 doctors, pharmacists, and scientists, mostly from academia but 2 from health plans and 1 from a large pharmaceutical firm.[21] The group was charged with performing a scientific function in a politically charged environment, with "special interests" pushing and pulling from every direction.

A model formulary would contain a number of drugs grouped according to their therapeutic applications and serve as a model for the individual plans—stipulating not which particular drugs to include, but specific therapeutic categories and the number of drugs within a given category. Obviously, such a model would arouse considerable interest among the different players. Drug makers wanted every drug to be in its own category, to ensure that the MGEC's model would result in plans including every one of their products. Conversely, the private health plans were interested in a small number of categories. A small number would mean that many drugs fit into a particular group, giving the plans leverage to negotiate with drug makers for discounts in exchange for designating "preferred" drugs to be members of those groups.

As USP's work proceeded, it became clear that for some drug categories in which all drugs were regarded as "therapeutically equivalent," only one drug would be needed to satisfy clinicians. But the pharmaceutical industry lobbied successfully, and the law requires that each category contain at least two drugs. When this news leaked to the media, tremendous controversy ensued. Everyone with a financial stake began to jockey for position. In fact, intense lobbying efforts on the part of the special interests had begun well before the passage of the legislation. The "final" USP model formulary included 146 drug categories and classes. The pharmaceutical firms had wanted 209; the health plans had sought 75. The model formulary's categories and classes each contained at least two drugs.[22]

As the debate about the formulary unfolded through press accounts, it seemed as though maintaining the financial security of the private healthcare industry was paramount, with patient needs secondary. There was nastiness, character assassination, swirling charges of conflict of interest by the parties with financial stakes in the outcome, and—in the midst of all this—the MGEC doing its very best to represent the interests of patients while staying within the general guidelines of Medicare Part D.

So, with the law enacted and the formulary set, how have things turned out? Are patients getting access to the medicines they need, when they need them? And will all of this lead to lower drug prices and tolerable costs to the government under Medicare?

## *Implementation Nightmares*

As with so many recent government programs, Medicare Part D's implementation was difficult. In fact, calling it a nightmare is no exaggeration. In the period leading up to January 1, 2006, when the benefit went into effect, through the May 15, 2006, enrollment deadline, the program lurched through one misstep after another. People had to sort through a "flood of advertising" and healthcare lobbying and try to understand confusing and varying drug plans (averaging forty for each state) so they could decide whether to give up a current healthcare plan under which they may have better coverage and select a private plan before incurring a financial late penalty. For senior citizens, this meant navigating a maze of "confusion and inertia" in an effort to weigh "the value of plans with different premiums, co-payments, deductibles, and lists of drugs that will be covered." Obtaining information was a key problem. Some came through mail and phone options were available, but online recommendations were impractical for many senior citizens— most of whom had never touched, much less owned, a computer. During the enrollment period, the news outlets were full of stories predicting that a large portion of people would end up paying a higher price than traditional Medicare, with only equal or even less benefits.[23]

The government's attempts at clarification fell flat. Online FAQs were far from helpful, and the government even admitted that its 2006 Medicare handbook was flawed and needed revision. Big delays in approving applications for the new Medicare drug benefit kept seniors from receiving the identification cards they needed to obtain prescriptions from pharmacists. Mental patients took the delays especially hard A psychiatric hospital in Jacksonville, Florida, reported an increase in admissions of patients unable to get medicines they had been taking for years. Many others patients, unable to obtain the medication they needed or significantly overcharged, simply panicked.[24]

The frenzied implementation of Medicare Part D clearly showed that the government was unprepared. New Hampshire Governor John Lynch called the program "a nightmare for many of our citizens." Forty-six state governments intervened in an effort to fix things, providing vital and greatly appreciated assistance for those unable to purchase their medications. Pharmacists also provided relief by distributing free prescriptions, but became frustrated as they remained unpaid by health plans and lost money. President Bush, hoping to alleviate the situation, told insurers to allow for a transition period and supply patients with a month's worth of medication until paperwork could be processed.[25]

By February 2006, doctors and pharmacists were complaining of conflicts with insurance companies, reporting that "many drugs theoretically covered by the new Medicare drug benefit are not readily available" due to "insurance restrictions and requirements." Many people were also stuck in two insurance plans as they attempted to make a switch, reporting more significant delays and frustration. These "enrollment discrepancies" only exacerbated problems. Then, to make matters worse, state officials accused President Bush of misleading people for political gain. CBS pulled Bush's television commercials, stating they violated a "longstanding policy on advocacy advertising," and the Government Accountability Office (GAO) found the administration's ads distorted benefits. Months later, the GAO also asserted that the Bush administration violated federal law by using tax dollars to produce and distribute what it called a type of "covert propaganda"— namely, a purportedly independent newscast intended to laud Medicare Part D.[26]

By mid-April 2006, the Kaiser Family Foundation reported that 46 percent of seniors viewed Medicare Part D unfavorably. Another Kaiser poll indicated that nearly half of the nation's elderly were not even aware of the May 15 deadline—only three weeks away—to sign up for the program. Officials had failed to notify confused seniors. The administration tweaked the system in an effort to get more senior citizens to join—creating, for example, a protection policy to ensure people could obtain the same drugs if their chosen program was altered. And then, as a bipartisan effort got underway to extend the deadline or waive penalty fees—with Democrats and Republicans alike arguing that a cut-off date served no purpose— President Bush refused. "Deadlines help people understand there's finality," he insisted, "and people need to get after it, you know?" Uncertainty with choices and options continued, though most seniors reached a final decision. By May, around 30 million Medicare recipients had some form of prescription coverage, with 8.1 million voluntarily enrolled in a freestanding drug program.[27]

Many were surprised at the large number of insurance companies that went on to offer drug plans under Medicare Part D. The private insurance industry seemed to have been handed a more appealing business opportunity than expected; previously, experts had "doubted that insurers would accept the risk of providing drug-only coverage to elderly and disabled people, because those with the highest costs would be the most likely to enroll." With promises of government subsidies as protection from loss, however, insurers began to view the program as a moneymaking proposition.

The pharmaceutical companies, too, seemed to gain from Medicare Part D. The HealthWell Foundation, among others, gives plan participants money to help make drug purchases. The main sponsors for this co-pay charity, however, are pharmaceutical companies, which provide "nearly all the money." Many fear that this is a manipulation of the system that allows the drug industry to keep prices high—patients will have enough to make the co-payment and insurance companies will pay for the majority of the drug. Medicare Part D has made these foundations "busier than ever."

For 2008, only a small percentage of drug plans will offer the standard benefit; most beneficiaries have tiered copayments. And while many people who never had any drug coverage now do, millions still find themselves forced to spend money in the coverage gap (the "doughnut hole").[28] It is very difficult to assess how many people are better off with Medicare Part D.

Overall, big business appeared to be the biggest winner—precisely because the current system makes it impossible to solve the problem of high prices and access while ensuring the ongoing innovation that is funded by those prices.[29] The important point is that even if implementation *had* gone smoothly, the law itself is flawed. Problem-free implementation would not have solved the fundamental problem that requires a new approach to address, simultaneously, the seemingly competing issues of access to needed drugs, high prices, and ongoing innovation.

## *What the Medicare Part D Experience Tells Us*

More time needs to pass before the full effects of the implementation of Medicare Part D can be understood. Many new dilemmas are arising. UnitedHealth Group and Humana, two prescription drug insurance providers, have acquired almost half of the market, potentially transforming the intended competitive market into an *oligopoly* that benefits only the powerful few. Creating an oligopoly is hardly a way to reduce prescription drug prices. It does mean that most elderly people will face the same small number of choices for their drug benefits that workers in most large companies face for their health insurance. By the same token, however, the large companies will have some clout as they bargain with the drug companies. The question is whether there will be any incentive for them to use it.[30]

A June 2006 paper in the *New England Journal of Medicine* suggests that Medicare Part D will be no more effective in reducing medical costs than it will be in lowering drug prices. Comparing consumers with drug benefits capped at $1,000 with consumers lacking any such cap, that study confirmed one part of the theory of managed competition: If people are faced with higher costs, they'll cut back on spending. It found that spending on drugs by consumers with the cap fell by 30 percent. But notably, the Journal's study found that *total* medical spending by these people did not fall. What happened? The decline in drug spending was completely offset by increases in other healthcare-related spending! These people, who weren't buying as many drugs, ended up going to emergency rooms more often. They had more non-elective hospitalizations and more of them died. Overall medical costs did not decline and those people whose drug benefits were capped clearly suffered.[31]

In other words, even if Medicare Part D ultimately succeeds in lowering spending on drugs, it is unlikely to lower total medical spending and even more unlikely to improve people's lives.

The main reason—if not the only reason—that the government acted on prescription drugs with Medicare Part D is because high drug prices are reducing access to medicines. But the government's actions do nothing to improve access to the premium-priced drugs discussed earlier.

> *Even if Medicare Part D ultimately succeeds in lowering spending on drugs, it is unlikely to lower total medical spending and even more unlikely to improve people's lives.*

Why should you expect access to future innovative drugs, which will be similarly priced, to be any different?

Drug prices promise to continue their rise. But even if some don't, and even if programs like Medicare Part D improve access to a small percentage of patients, whatever good effects the government's actions have on drug costs seem to distort other healthcare costs and cause them to go up. The situation cries out for a solution that provides access to drugs for those who need them *and* maintains the financial incentives for continued innovation.

Americans face a kind of Catch-22, as reflected in the debate leading up to passage of Medicare Part D. Some argued then that allowing the government to negotiate lower prices would solve the access problem. But at what cost? Under the current system, the pharmaceutical companies would surely have realized less revenue, and cuts in spending on drug discovery and development would have surely followed. The risk was to cut off the flow of new innovations, and hamper the overall economic benefits and prestige that accompany having the world's greatest pharmaceutical industry.

Simply lowering out-of-pocket payments, while keeping prices high, created the huge cost of Medicare Part D—and, as we already pointed out, someone has to pay the difference.

We're left with a program that continues to climb in costs to taxpayers, while leaving many elderly no better off than before and some even worse off than they were before Medicare Part D. Meanwhile, the drug companies continue to do well—because the system is set up to ensure that they have large revenues so they can continue to make scientific advances.

So, is a market-driven system like this, with no changes in how the pharmaceutical industry does business, likely to reduce prescription drug prices or at least keep them in check? The evidence suggests the contrary. Similar incentives have existed for more than a decade in employer-based health plans that offer drug coverage, and the large drug firms have simply adjusted their marketing strategies to these changes in the environment. We haven't seen any evidence of drug prices coming down as a result. Rather, over the past 10 years of employer health plans commonly offering formularies with tiered co-payments for medicines, prices of drugs have gone up, not down, at rate increases of 5 or 6 percent. Such increases even outstrip the overall inflation rate.[32]

Clearly, something must be done. If the current system doesn't allow for a solution to rising drug prices *and* a way to ensure that we continue to enjoy the benefits of pharmaceutical innovation, then we need some very new thinking. Might a new way to use research and development resources point the way?

## *Endnotes*

[1] Gordon, G. 2000. Congress takes on drug prices; the national debate can be traced to Minnesota seniors who are fed up with risings costs. *Minneapolis-St. Paul Star Tribune*, July 24:1A.

[2] Wolfe, W. 1995. Prescription drugs cost much less in Canada, seniors say. *Minneapolis-St. Paul Star Tribune*, July 26:2B.

[3] Chicago Sun-Times. 1999. Study targets seniors' medicine cost. *Chicago Sun-Times*, October 25:3.

[4] Barry, E. 2000. Drug lifeline runs north. *Boston Globe*, April 11:B1. See also: Goldberg, C. 2000. Maine will cap drug prices with a groundbreaking law. *New York Times*, April 12. See also: Davis, K. 2003. Drug score. *Kiplinger's Personal Finance* (February). See also: Goldberg, C. 2000a. Maine enacts a law aimed at controlling costs of drugs. *New York Times*, May 12:A30. See also: Noonan, D. 2000. The real drug war. *Newsweek*, May 8:28.

[5] Davis, K. 2004. Is it safe? *Kiplinger's Personal Finance*, (July. See also: Goldberg, Carey. 2000b. Drug maker fires back at Maine over law. *New York Times*, August 4: A12. See also: Mishra, R. 2000. Trailblazers elders' effort led to Maine drug law. *Boston Globe*, August 21:A1.

[6] Pear, R. 2003. Medicare chief joins firm with health clients. *New York Times*, December 19:A34. See also: Goldstein, A. 2004. Official says he was told to withhold medicare data. *Washington Post*, March 13:A1.

[7] Pear, R. 2005. Bush vows veto of any cutback in drug benefit. *New York Times*, February 12:A1.

[8] While Enthoven recognized the link between technology and aging and rising healthcare costs, he believed that these factors could or should not be changed. See: Enthoven, A. C. 1978. Consumer-choice health plan (first of two parts)—Inflation and inequity in health care today: Alternatives for cost control and an analysis of proposals for national health insurance. *New England Journal of Medicine* 298:12, 650–58. See also: Enthoven, A. C. 1978. Consumer-choice health plan (second of two parts)—A national health-insurance proposal based on regulated competition in the private sector. *New England Journal of Medicine* 298:13, 709–720. See also: Enthoven, A. C. 1980. *Health Plan: The Only Practical Solution to the Soaring Cost of Medical Care*. Reading, Mass.: Addison-Wesley, xvi–xvii. Emphasis in original.

[9] Moss, David A. 2002. *When All Else Fails: Government as the Ultimate Risk Manager*. Cambridge, Mass.: Harvard University Press.

[10] Enthoven, 1980, *op. cit.* See also: Ellwood, P. M., A. C. Enthoven, and L. Etheredge. 1992. The Jackson Hole Initiatives for a twenty-first century American healthcare system. *Health Economics* 1:3, 149–168.

[11] Arrow, 1963, *op. cit.*

[12] Maxwell, J. and P. Temin. 2002. Managed competition versus industrial purchasing of health care among the Fortune 500. *Journal of Health Politics, Policy, and Law* 27:1, 5–30. Enthoven has acknowledged that managed competition has not been tried. He argued in 2002 that increases in the cost of health care showed that the Fortune 500 model has not worked either. He remains convinced that managed competition could work in two senses. First, businesses and people would adopt it and it would reduce the growth of medical expenditures. After 25 years of inability of managed competition to do either, Enthoven's faith is impressive. See: Enthoven, A. C. 2002. Commentary—the Fortune 500 model for health care: Is now the time to change? *Journal of Health Politics, Policy, and Law* 27:1, 37–48.

[13] Swenson, P. and S. Greer. 2002. Foul weather friends: Big business and healthcare reform in the 1990s in historical perspective. *Journal of Health Politics, Policy, and Law* 27:4, 605.

[14] Pear, R. 2003a. Bush to propose sweeping changes in Medicare plan. *New York Times* (January 3): A1. See also: Pear, R. 2003b. Plan to overhaul Medicare by enlarging private health plan role is criticized. *New York Times*, May 6:A28.

[15] Pear, R. 2006. Medicare beneficiaries confused and angry over gap in drug coverage. *New York Times*, July 30:14.

[16] Feldstein, Martin S. 1981. *Hospital Costs and Health Insurance*. Cambridge, Mass.: Harvard University Press.

[17] Berenson, A. 2006. Drug plan's side effect is severe. *New York Times*, April 8:C1.

[18] Darc, K. 2006. "Going to have to sell my house . . . or die": Medicare drug plan gap has some paying dearly. *San Diego Union-Tribune*, July 16:H1. See also:

Wolf, R. 2006. More patients fall into a hole in drug benefit; many on Medicare surprised by the costly gap in coverage. *USA Today,* July 27:4A.

[19] Pear, R. 2007. Bill to let Medicare negotiate drug prices is blocked. *New York Times,* April 18.

[20] Gaynor, M., J. Li and W. B. Vogt. 2006. Is drug coverage a free lunch? Cross-price elasticities and the design of prescription drug benefits. National Bureau of Economic Research, Working Paper no. 12758. See also: Horn S. D., P. D. Sharkey, and C. Phillips-Harris. 1998. Formulary limitations and the elderly: Results from the Managed Care Outcomes Project. *American Journal of Managed Care* 4:8, 1105–1113. See also: Horn S. D., P. D. Sharkey, D. M. Tracy, C. E. Horn, B. James, and F. Goodwin. 1996. Intended and unintended consequences of HMO cost-containment strategies: Results from the Managed Care Outcomes Project. *American Journal of Managed Care* 2:3, 253–264. See also: Huskamp, H. A., R. G. Frank, K. A. McGuigan, and Y. Zhang. 2005. The impact of a three-tier formulary on demand response for prescription drugs. *Journal of Economics and Management Strategy* 14:3, 729. See also: Soumerai, S. B., J. Avorn, D. Ross-Degnan, and S. Gortmaker. 1987. Payment restrictions for prescription drugs under Medicaid: Effects on therapy, cost, and equity. *New England Journal of Medicine* 317:9, 550–56. See also: Soumerai, S. B., D. Ross-Degnan, J. Avorn, T. J. McLaughlin, and I. Choodnovskiy. 1991. Effects of Medicaid drug-payment limits on admission to hospitals and nursing homes. *New England Journal of Medicine* 325:15, 1072–77. See also: Crown, W. H., E. R. Berndt, O. Baser, S. N. Finkelstein, W. P. Witt, J. Maguire, and K. E. Haver. 2004. Benefit plan design and prescription drug utilization among asthmatics: Do patient co-payments matter? *NBER/Frontiers in Health Policy Research* 7:1, 95.

[21] It should be noted that one of the authors, Stan N. Finkelstein, served on this expert panel.

[22] The USP Model Guidelines Expert Committee and U.S. Pharmacopeia Staff. 2006. Narrative review: The U.S. Pharmacopeia and Model Guidelines for Medicare Part D Formularies. *Annals of Internal Medicine* 145:448–453.

[23] New York Times Editors. 2005. Drug coverage in the face of deficits. *New York Times*, October 2. See also: Pear, R. 2005a. Get ready: Medicare drug plan's to-do list. *New York Times,* April 12:G2.

[24] Boston Herald Editorial Staff. 2005. Drug plan worth the pain. *Boston Herald,* November 15:34. See also: Pear, R. 2005b. Medicare will revise guide to new benefits for 2006. *New York Times,* May 22:26. See also: Pear, R. 2006a. Medicare woes take high toll on mentally ill. *New York Times,* January 21:A1.

[25] Pear, R. 2006b. Pharmacists say drug plan threatens their livelihood. *New York Times,* March 13:A12. See also: Pear, R. 2006c. President tells insurers to aid new drug plan. *New York Times,* January 16:A1. See also: Pear, R. 2006d. States Intervene after drug plan hits early snags. *New York Times,* January 8:A1.

26 Pear, R. 2004. A watchdog sees flaws in Bush's ads on Medicare. *New York Times*, March 11:A26; Pear, R. 2004a. CBS pulls advertisement on Medicare prepared by administration. *New York Times*, February 14:A20. See also: Pear, R. 2006e. In Medicare maze, some find they're tangled in two drug plans. *New York Times*, March 1:A1. See also: Pear, R. 2006f. Rules of Medicare drug plans slow access to benefits. *New York Times*, February 14:A17. See also: Pear, R. 2004b. Ruling says White House's Medicare videos were illegal. *New York Times*, May 20:A24.

27 Kaiser Family Foundation. 2006. Public opinion on Medicare Part D—the Medicare prescription drug benefit. *Health Poll Report Survey* (conducted April 6–11, 2006). www.kff.org/spotlight/medicarerx/index.cfm (accessed April 21, 2007). See also: Krugman, P. 2006. D for debacle. *New York Times*, May 15:A21. See also: Pear, R. 2006g. Deadline near, jams are seen for drug plan. *New York Times*, April 24:A1. See also: Pear, R. 2006h. Medicare rule guarantees continuity of drugs. *New York Times*, April 27:A14. See also: Wolf, R. 2006a. Many seniors unaware of deadline for Medicare drug plan. *USA Today*, April 26:8A.

28 The Henry J. Kaiser Foundation. October 2007. Medicare fact sheet—the Medicare prescription drug benefit. http://www.kff.org/medicare/upload/7044_07.pdf (accessed November 2, 2007).

29 Pear, R. 2005c. Defying experts, insurers join Medicare drug plan. *New York Times*, March 6:A1. See also: Berenson, A. 2006a. In drug-aid foundations, a web of corporate interests. *New York Times*, April 8:C4.

30 Pear, R. 2006i. In scramble for new Medicare business, a few insurers grab the most. *New York Times*, April 29:A8.

31 Hsu, J., M. Price, *et al.* 2006. Unintended consequences of caps on Medicare drug benefits. *New England Journal of Medicine* 354:22, 2349–2359.

32 American Association of Retired Persons. 2006. Trends in manufacturer prices of brand name prescription drugs used by older Americans—first quarter 2006 update. AARP Public Policy Institute. http://assets.aarp.org/rgcenter/health/dd140_drugprices.pdf (accessed April 22, 2007).

# CHAPTER SIX

## SQUANDERING R & D RESOURCES

*It isn't that they can't see the solution. It's that they can't see the problem.*

—G.K. Chesterton

The system through which medicines make it to the market in the Unites States has gone terribly awry. It's not just that the big successes of the 1980s and 1990s in developing blockbuster drugs are not sustainable, as the drought in new drugs approved by the FDA reveals. It's not just that the "low-hanging fruit has been picked" or that the easy drugs have already been developed. No, the problem is much more serious.

The system certainly does not lack resources. Collectively, drug firms spend tens of billions of dollars each year on research. The National Science Foundation estimated spending at $31 billion in 2004; according to the pharmaceutical industry itself, the figure reached $51.3 billion in 2005.[1] The difference has to do with how the amounts are calculated, but in either case there's no denying that a lot of money goes into research. In fact, the pharmaceutical industry spends more on research than just about any other industry in the United States; only computer and electronics firms spend similar amounts.

There's surely no shortage of illnesses to target for drug R & D. The world is full of medical problems just waiting to be solved. Not too long ago, though, the CEO of one of the large European-based multinational pharmaceutical firms told an MIT audience that he didn't know what to do with all of the money in his research budget. How could someone not know what to do with all that money, especially someone in the pharmaceutical industry? The answer lies in the fact that the boundary between scientific decisions and business decisions has become blurred, a situation today that amounts to putting profit-seeking ahead of good science. Our broken system *encourages* it.

Those who try to maximize profits and shareholder value are acting no differently than their counterparts in any other industry. But this *isn't* any other industry. It's health care and pharmaceuticals—and the stakes are enormous. Decisions can mean life or, in the case of drugs like Vioxx, death. And society bears much of the cost.

Consider the following hypothetical interchange between a doctor and her patient who suffers from severe nasal allergies. Just as the doctor walks in, the patient begins to sneeze incessantly. Then he's finally able to speak. "I take my non-sedating antihistamine every day during allergy season, but I still sneeze like this. I used to take Benadryl, but it made me drowsy. This new drug doesn't make me sleepy, but it sure doesn't fully relieve my symptoms."

"Interesting," the doctor replies. "I recruited patients for a clinical trial of one of the non-sedating antihistamines. As I recall, trial subjects were asked to rate their reduction in the sedating effects, but nothing about whether their sneezing and runny noses were less frequent. And I've heard from some colleagues that their patients who take a double dose daily—twice the FDA-approved dose—report much better symptom relief but also get drowsy."

"Then why did the FDA approve the smaller dose?" asks the patient.

"I don't know what the FDA was thinking," the doctor answers, "but I can tell you that doctors and the drug company have a lot of leeway in these trials. All the company had to do was get it to market in the lower dose and then mount a huge advertising campaign about its new breakthrough drug that doesn't make you drowsy. Of course, it's illegal for the drug company to promote the higher dose, but not for doctors to prescribe it."

"Yeah," says the patient. "If I had taken the higher dose of the non-sedating antihistamine to begin with, why would it matter if I switched from Benadryl?"

The doctor nods. "Good point."

"But doc," he continues, "I'm curious about this leeway business. Apparently *you* can tell me to take a double dose if you think I should. I take this medication for something that just annoys me— hay fever. What about the Lipitor you have me taking? Isn't that for something more 'life or death'?"

Lipitor is one of the world's largest-selling medications. It's one of the *statin drugs,* which are prescribed to lower cholesterol in order to reduce the risk of heart disease. Millions of people all over the world take these medicines safely. A lot of doctors and patients regard them as "lifelong" pills. It's medicine you'll take until you die, which—if the drug works—won't be from heart disease. "Look," says the doctor, "Lipitor is really potent. The manufacturer initially tested it at a relatively low dosage, and the results showed that it produced more cholesterol reduction at a lower dose than its main competitors did at a somewhat higher dose. Now there's a company-sponsored study I just read in the *New England Journal of Medicine* that reports even higher doses of Lipitor do an even better job in so-called 'high-risk' patients.[2] The company won't be unhappy if doctors prescribe Lipitor at these higher doses for lots of patients who are at 'normal' risk. I've prescribed the typical dose for you, but I'm sure some doctors will ask themselves: 'Why take a chance?'

"They can do that?" the patient exclaims in disbelief.

"Absolutely," the doctor assures him, "and with virtually no risk of sanction by the FDA."

We wish we could assure you that this kind of mischief with doses was the only problem with our system. In fact, though, there's a whole litany.

## *Working a Broken System*

Remember, drug development is a business. The first obligation of the firms is to their shareholders, just as in any other business. Take a look at what we like to call the "Five Unwritten Rules of Successful Drug Development" under the current system, and you'll see what we mean.

The first rule is this: Develop only drugs that have *paying* markets, where a nice revenue stream can come from either lots of people with the disease or high prices, or both.

No private company is compelled to develop any particular drug, no matter how badly society needs it. Despite all the great advances that have been made in therapeutic medicines, science today seems to play second fiddle to business considerations. When Merck's animal division came up with a drug effective against a broad variety of parasites in cattle, horses, pigs, sheep, and dogs, the company was thrilled; animal owners spend a lot of money on medications to prevent parasitic problems. But then someone at the company recognized that the heartworm drug would work in humans to cure onchocerciasis. You'd think this would be a no-brainer: This drug will help large numbers of people, so go for it. But Merck was confronted with a *business* problem.

With *onchocerciasis*, parasitic worms that can live for up to 14 years in the human body infect its host and cause severe itching, lesions, and eventually blindness. The condition is so common in some African villages that children believe the symptoms to be a normal part of growing up. The disease is more commonly known as river blindness, because the worm breeds in fast-flowing rivers. So, how does this disease present a business problem to Merck?

These rivers are in west and central Africa—not exactly a paying market.[3]

If Merck agonized over whether to invest in developing the drug, it wasn't due to lack of excitement over the prospect of a cure for river blindness, but because of the company's fiduciary responsibility to its shareholders. Some 99 percent of the roughly 18 million people infected with river blindness live in Africa and do not have the wherewithal to purchase the medicine. It was completely legitimate for the company's business people to remind decision makers that Merck is not a charity.

In this instance, which has become a famous Harvard Business School case study, the company decided to proceed, calculating that its scientists—many of whom were in the doldrums because of unrelated problems at Merck—would be encouraged by the decision and that the positive public relations would be good for the firm. In the end, Merck donated and distributed the finished product at no profit. The success of the company's antiparasitic drug for animals, which was making more than $300 million each year and on which the river blindness drug was based, no doubt made the decision easier. But if only the narrowest business considerations had been factored in, this drug might never have made it to the millions who benefit![4]

The second rule: Mount clinical trials that target any health problem that you are certain will get the drug to market in the shortest time or with the fewest number of patients in the trials. Once that hurdle has been passed, other uses will be found for the drug—often without the need to do any further clinical testing. After all, off label prescribing is perfectly legal. If you can just get into that paying market, the business side of the house can take care of the rest.

Third, test the *lowest* dosage of the drug that will show any benefit to patients. We already gave some examples. The FDA will be happy if the lowest possible dosage is the one proposed and, better yet, you can make even more money after the drug is on the market.

Just produce a new study showing that a higher dose yields better results in some patients.[5]

Fourth, take advantage of every opportunity the system affords to craft clinical trials that serve your business interests. For instance, academic doctors can be useful to conduct clinical trials, but don't use them unless you really need to. Their university bureaucracies move slowly, and worse, they'll probably insist on publishing the results even if the trials show that the drug doesn't work well. Many contract research organizations, though, will publish only if you tell them to. Don't worry if the trials find that the drug is not particularly efficacious. As long as it works for some people, and you can get it on the market, the revenue will add up. There are always plenty of people who try but fail to benefit, and each and every one of them is a paying customer (either with or without insurance). And, by the way, clinical trials also provide excellent opportunities to pay doctors to try the medicines on their patients.[6]

Fifth, and most important, never forget to price the drug as high as the market will bear. Don't leave money on the table.

This is the system we have, but not a single one of these five rules is required in order to get new drugs. In fact, only three essential components are needed to develop a new medicine.

- Plenty of money for the development of new medicines

- World-class, cutting-edge scientific research

- Some kind of incentives to engage in drug development

What about getting the *right* drugs—the ones society needs most? What is essential in a new system that replaces our broken one to ensure that we *continue* to get innovative drug therapies and that they are accessible and affordable for all who need them? The answer is largely the same: money, world-class science, and incentives. But the incentives must serve a different purpose: align choices about which drugs to develop with what society truly needs.

Through the 1990s, great successes in drug development resulted because the first two of these essential elements kept the innovation engine running, and there was just enough overlap of market considerations with societal needs to get the "right" drugs to market. But now we're seeing a drought in new drugs, rising costs, and growing access problems. The situation promises only to worsen if we don't fix the system. Continued innovations—and hence medical advancements—are at stake.

Let's take a look at each of these components—money, science, and incentives—to set the stage for our proposed solution. First, the money.

## So Much Money, So Badly Used

The first essential component to making sure we have great medicines is financial: There needs to be plenty of funding to invest in drug development. The good news is that *the money's there*. In fact, as explained earlier, the pharmaceutical companies not only have plenty of money and enjoy profits that are the envy of other industries, but they conduct their business in an environment largely free of financial risk at the company level. The profit-making machine just keeps chugging along.

The decades after World War II were an exciting time to work in the pharmaceutical industry. Drug

*Pharmaceutical companies not only have plenty of money and enjoy profits that are the envy of other industries, but they conduct their business in an environment largely free of financial risk at the company level. The profit-making machine just keeps chugging along.*

companies easily attracted high-quality scientists—first chemists and, much later, biologists—to jobs with a practical mission: Find new drug therapies and bring them to market. The resources in academia were easily trumped by what was offered in the private sector: big budgets, considerable leeway in how you spent your research dollars, and no stringently constructed grant proposals to write. Revenues, especially as blockbusters entered the market, were more than ample for the big pharmaceutical companies to keep pouring resources into R & D—so ample, in fact, that *cost-efficient* drug discovery was barely on the radar screen before the early 1990s.

The big pharmaceutical companies could spend money with near impunity when it came to R & D. When one of the authors was in medical school in the 1970s, a drug firm offered summer positions to a large number of people in his class. The company had offices in several Northeast locations, and on weekends the classmates working at these different sites would often take camping trips together. One student working in drug discovery showed up with steaks, and everyone agreed they were some of the best and freshest they'd ever tasted. Asked how he could afford to bring all this high-quality food, the student replied that he worked for a scientist in the company who did animal studies. Whenever this scientist placed an order for study subjects, he would order extra cattle and slaughter them for steaks. There was, as the saying goes, money to burn.

To this day, the big pharmaceutical companies enjoy enviable financial resources. So, should we worry about the financial picture? Absolutely. In a defective system, the fact that there's plenty of money around doesn't mean it's being spent wisely. In fact, we believe these resources—which are certainly not limitless—are being squandered. Plus, bad financial decisions invite the kind of scrutiny that could lead to government intervention of the kind that *halts* rather than promotes innovation.

Drug development is tremendously costly. As discussed in Chapter 1, "Drugs and Drug Prices," the most widely reported statistic (from Tufts) of the average cost to develop each new pre-scription chemical (or "small molecule") drug and bring it to market is nearly $900 million dollars. For biological drugs (like vaccines and antibodies), its $1.2 billion. These figures include not only the direct expenses for scientific work and clinical trials of ultimately *successful* drug candidates—the ones that make it to market—but also all the money spent on every other drug candidate that proved unsafe or didn't alleviate symptoms of disease. In addition, the estimate accounts for *opportunity costs*, meaning the difference between what the drug company earns using its money for drug development (which may fail) and what it *could* have earned if that money had financed an alternative investment that generated a higher return.[7]

## CALCULATING THE COST OF DRUG DEVELOPMENT IS AN IMPERFECT SCIENCE

Figuring out the real cost of drug development is fraught with diffi-culties, and there are certainly some imperfections in the estimate we cite. For instance, the figure from the Tufts University Center for the Study of Drug Development suffers from its reliance on self-reported information by drug companies about their *in-house* development efforts, while excluding costs associated with acquisitions by large companies of the drugs discovered and/or developed by smaller firms. Those acquisition costs may be inflated for a host of reasons, and the final acquisition price often reflects not only the real market value of what's being purchased but also whatever bidding inflation is necessary to be competitive and, sometimes, to acquire an entire firm and not just its one promising molecule. Also, within the small firms the cost of drug development may be very different. A small biotechnology firm, spun off from university research, has nowhere near the resources of a Merck or Pfizer, so it has no choice but to be more efficient in its work. Most likely, venture capitalists are scrutinizing every move. And since the smaller firms tend to have fewer development projects, the price of the failure of one molecule can often be the demise of the entire company.

Whatever the real cost of drug development—and remember, the number reflects both the successes and failures—no one argues that it isn't extraordinarily high. Hundreds of millions of dollars are needed to bring a new drug to market. That's a tough investment to recoup, which drives the blockbuster mentality we've been talking about. It's a vicious circle. The drug companies need top-selling drugs in order to earn back their huge financial investment. The only way to find those blockbusters involves testing tens of thousands of other drug candidates—including some that might offer promise to patient populations much smaller than the investment and eventual payoff warrants, but *medically* valuable nonetheless.

Also, the competition for both public and private investment funds leads firms, especially comparatively resource-poor smaller firms, to race through clinical trial stages, often advancing to the next stage when results are questionable. This, too, affects the overall cost of drug development. The result is resources wasted on drugs that don't succeed. And worse, even when drug candidates are thoroughly tested in clinical trials, problems can still arise later—like what we described with Vioxx. Some toxic effects show up only after a drug has been on the market and taken by large numbers of people for a period of years.

On top of this enormous cost, there's big financial risk—and the price of bearing that risk is built into the high cost Americans pay for drugs. It's not risk at the company level; we showed earlier that such risk doesn't really exist for the large pharmaceutical firms. The risk we're talking about here is at the level of the molecule. Drug development itself is *very* risky, which contributes to the overall cost of drug development and, in turn, to the high prices we end up paying.

You need to understand how drug development has traditionally worked to grasp the full nature of this risk. The typical process of finding a new drug involves the random screening of some 10,000 molecules in the search for anything that shows promise. For each 10,000 molecules screened, one marketable drug might emerge. We don't know whether the 10,000 number is truly accurate, but it's clear that the process has a low likelihood of finding a marketable molecule. And if any new chemical entity has only a slim chance of becoming a successful drug, a very high risk is incurred.

Drug development, though, is changing. One of the main changes has to do with lead optimization, which was discussed earlier. As technology enables more efficient drug discovery, scientists use computers to make incremental changes to molecular structures and several million molecules. Yet, even with a better understanding of the mechanisms of drug action, advanced technology, and millions of molecular forms being screened, fewer successful drugs are created.

Given such a small probability of success, investing in any particular candidate drug at the early stages is risky. The costs involved for the overwhelming majority of drugs that are unsuccessful *must* be distributed among all those that do succeed in getting to market. Some fail early, so the costs incurred are relatively low, but others don't fail until the clinical trials phase, after tens or perhaps hundreds of millions have been spent. The opportunity costs, in particular, make the delays in bringing drugs to market so costly, and compel the pharmaceutical firms to be in such a hurry to launch them to market. It can take as long as 15 to 20 years from the time a promising molecule is found until a single cent can be recouped through sales. On average, that translates into *huge* opportunity costs.

One study, after "adding up" all candidates and stages of the drug-development process, claims that a candidate drug has *only about a 13 percent* overall likelihood of emerging from screening and actually making it all the way to FDA approval. Once the drug gets to market, the risk continues. Another study finds that only around one-third of all newly introduced drugs earn more than the average cost incurred for R & D, with the top 10 percent alone accounting for half of all earnings. Therefore, distributing risks among all drug candidates from the beginning of the process is critical to ensure that the large probability of failure is compensated with the few highly profitable successes.[8]

---

## How Researchers Determined the Low Probability of a Drug Making It to Market

The MIT researchers who determined that drugs have a 13 percent chance of making it to market estimated the proportion of drug candidates successfully passing each individual stage of drug development. These are the risk numbers they came up with for each drug that emerges from initial screening as having confirmed biological activity:

- That the drug candidate is suitable as a human drug (in technical parlance, has satisfactory ADMET—adsorption, distribution, metabolism and excretion properties, and toxicity): 60 percent.

- That the drug candidate then survives pre-clinical testing: 90 percent.

- That the drug then survives the three phases of clinical testing: 75 percent, 50 percent, and 85 percent, respectively.

- That the drug, once all testing is completed, wins FDA approval: 75 percent.

Multiplying all of these probabilities together ($0.6 \times 0.9 \times 0.75 \times 0.5 \times 0.85 \times 0.75 = 0.13$) results in the *overall* probability of getting a successful drug from all the candidates at the beginning—13 percent.

---

One of the largest single drivers of the still-rising cost of developing drugs is the way in which clinical trials are conducted. In many ways, the issues surrounding clinical trials are a microcosm of an overall and pressing problem that gets in the way of access to needed medicines at affordable prices: *business encroaching on science*. In our broken pharmaceutical system, the problem isn't just that money may be spent unwisely. It's also that it often ends up being spent in ways that compromise the best possible scientific work—all with unspoken FDA approval.

## *Business Encroaches on Our World-Class Science*

The implementation of the 1962 drug amendments established clinical trials to be the standard for evaluating new drug candidates for safety and efficacy. The pre-market testing that evolved for human clinical trials involves several phases:

- Phase I: Study a drug's safety

- Phase II: Establish the efficacy of treatment in a trial of modest sample size

- Phase III: Confirm what you've learned so far using large numbers of subjects.

Integrated drug firms originally developed the in-house capability to manage trials through all three phases, often collaborating with medical schools where an abundance of clinical experts reside and where patients can be recruited. The focus was rigorous scientific investigation.[9]

In drug development today, business considerations are at least as likely as scientific ones to drive the design of the studies. All too often, today's drug studies are mounted as a way to get drugs into doctors' hands as quickly as possible so that doctors will try the drugs out on their patients. In fact, most studies are now conducted directly for the drug companies by doctors functioning as private entrepreneurs, rather than in collaboration with university medical centers. Sales and marketing are key motivators of these changes. But the open exchange of scientific information that emerges from the trials and that is so critical to future innovation is lost as a result.

Consider one drug maker that mounted an after-market study of a new use for a drug that had previously received FDA approval at a much lower dosage to treat an unrelated but highly prevalent disease. The new use was for cancer patients who would require much larger doses. Clinical trial findings that established the drug's value led, as expected, to FDA approval for the new use. But the drug firm, not yet finished with its "studies," next recruited a set of academic opinion leaders who were actively seeking new approaches to treating cancer, and then a group of practicing oncologists throughout the United States. A study protocol was produced that specified the dose and frequency of administration. Forms used to collect data about patients' experiences at specified intervals were distributed. But apparently no plans were made to submit these new data to the FDA, and little effort was made to enforce the study's rules. Rather, the effort seemed to be a market seeding study to get doctors to try out the medicine with their patients.

The company's expectations rose when results suggested that new cancer patient users enjoyed disproportionate improvements in "quality of life" compared to others. But the statistical analyses weren't robust enough, because too many patient records lacked all the data that were to have been collected. So, the drug company hired consultants and their affiliated academic economists and physicians to *infer* values for the "missing" data, using techniques similar to those for which James Heckman and Daniel McFadden earned the 2000 Nobel Prize in Economics. Later, the drug company presented this "enhanced" analysis to the FDA and advocated for changes in the drug's label, permitting a claim of better quality of life. But wouldn't the medical industry benefit more if they had designed a *proper* clinical trial in the first place?

Earlier, we described another way that drug manufacturers manipulate the design of clinical trials to maximize future revenues:

performing studies at low dosage levels. This is an all-too-common practice for companies that have invested a lot in a particular drug-development program and want to get the drug to market quickly. First they study a dosage level that will result in the fewest problems and thus win the quickest FDA approval. Once the FDA approves a drug for one indication, there's time to do what's needed to get other indications approved. Meanwhile, the drug company, although it cannot lawfully promote a new drug's off label uses, can be confident that many prescribers will know what the real objective was with the drug.

Testing a low dose and winning approval paves the way for showing later on that a higher dose is more beneficial. And there's an added benefit: If the price for the low dose has been set at, say, 75 cents per pill, then why not price a triple dose for another indication two or three times higher?

To ensure the primacy of business considerations in clinical trials, drug firms have moved the setting of their trials. Academic medical centers, one of the sources of innovative research that has helped advance drug development, were a natural choice to perform clinical trials when the process was first mandated. But in the mid-1980s, the FDA began to demand larger clinical trials, which meant more patients were needed. The academic institutions couldn't recruit fast enough. Soon, they turned to the newly formed small businesses called Contract Research Organizations (CROs) that were discussed earlier. CROs offered the integrated drug firms the possibility of outsourcing the recruitment of doctors and human subjects for their trials. CROs went even further, though; one of their important contributions was to monitor the quality of work of participating doctors as they followed the specified rules of the trials' research protocols.[10]

Over time, as part of what has been called the "industrialization of clinical research," this shift to CROs has resulted in a major move of clinical trials to community hospitals and other privately owned facilities.[11] From a business perspective, the shift offers all sorts of benefits to drug firms. They avoid the costs and delays associated with university bureaucracies and—most important—they gain greater control over the study's design. As one analyst describes the situation in today's pharmaceutical industry, "The medical needs of patients and scientific opportunities as they emerge from an open process of scientific enquiry have become secondary considerations."[12]

In 1994, some 75 percent of drug company-sponsored clinical trials were done in collaboration with academic medical centers.[13] By 2004, this number had declined to only 38 percent.[14] Also, rather than use cost-based research contracts, drug companies—now have doctors participating in clinical trials who are compensated via fees they are paid for each patient they recruit for a study. At a time when doctors' incomes from their clinical practices came under the pressure wrought by managed competition and reduced Medicare payments, this monetary incentive to participate in clinical trials and recruit patients points again to how business has encroached on science. According to a 1999 series of articles in the *New York Times*, doctors practicing in community settings who had not been active researchers started to receive funding and get authorship of articles in exchange for participating in pharmaceutical company-sponsored clinical trials.[15]

Abuses by groups executing trials and analyzing data are widely known in the medical community. For instance, important clients often insisted on adding the names of well-known physicians as "contributors" in professional journals in addition to the names of CRO staff and affiliated academic economists and physicians who provided data analysis services and authored manuscripts. Even though they hadn't been involved in the research, these doctors met the journals' minimum requirements for authorship. Clients would then engage these prestigious authors to present findings at professional meetings and company-sponsored events. Leading medical journals, however, in light of public scrutiny and controversy, have changed their rules and now require prospective authors to sign statements specifying their specific roles in the research.[16]

Still another area where business has encroached on science is "cost-benefit analysis." After consumers began to demand proof that the drugs they were purchasing were worth what the companies charged, drug firms turned to academics and asked them to use tools they had developed to evaluate the effectiveness of medical technologies and practices in terms of their costs. If they could quantify the benefits of a medication in dollars, which might include avoiding other kinds of costs such as doctor visits or hospitalizations, the companies reasoned they could make high prices more palatable to consumers. But when relatively few medicines were found to offset other direct medical costs, drug makers engaged behavioral scientists and other experts to develop surveys to demonstrate improved quality of life or productivity from drug treatments, hoping to translate these benefits into dollar terms. And once these drug cost-benefit or cost-effectiveness studies became commodities, they were again outsourced to CROs so drug makers could more readily control the results. The cost of doing such studies gets tacked on to the overall cost of developing a new drug. Eventually, even the respected, peer-reviewed journals began to realize that these studies were self-serving for the pharmaceutical industry.

## *Withholding Unfavorable Study Results from the Public*

What compels drug firms to shift the setting of clinical trials, outsource important analyses, create phantom authors, and work hard to ensure that scientific data that may be unfavorable for a drug is suppressed? *Control* is key—remember, this is business as well as science—and pharmaceutical companies take full advantage of a system that allows them to influence the outcome of studies.

A drug company's desire to control research parameters coincides with its financial incentive to hide unfavorable study results from investors and the public. While most companies are happy, for instance, to publish findings that a new drug offers significant clinical benefits, unfettered academic researchers might want to see *any* results appear in the public domain. But this concept runs contrary to business considerations.

> *A drug company's desire to control research parameters coincides with its financial incentive to hide unfavorable study results from investors and the public.*

"The focus on projected sales rather than on the scientific novelty and the medical value of the drugs and, in particular, the obsession with blockbusters, has compromised the creative potential and the innovative power of most big pharma companies," writes one analyst. "[B]ig pharma companies are increasingly choosing to be development and marketing machines rather than centers of innovative research."[17] And when that happens, when business encroaches on science, when the cost of drug discovery is high and shareholders are clamoring for profits, it's no wonder that drug companies find themselves compromising the integrity of their research before and after discovering new drugs.

## DO INVESTORS PUT PRESSURE ON CLINICAL TRIALS?

When Centocor did clinical testing for *Centoxin*, a drug that would have revolutionized treatment for *sepsis* (an often fatal complication of bacterial infections among hospitalized patients), some observers thought the results were equivocal. But Centocor went forward. Other firms have come up against compelling scientific evidence that a drug may not offer the promise once believed, and still decided to proceed to the next phase. In every case, it's business trumping science. The business people are loath to abandon a potential drug in which so much has already been invested. The losses mount and society suffers because overall drug costs, which are linked to the development efforts of *all* successful and failed drugs, increase to compensate for the money lost by virtue of the business decision. In this particular case, Centoxin made it to the European market, but was later withdrawn.[18]

Conversely, early scientific successes with promising new treatments not only are published in scientific journals, but are also reported to Wall Street stock analysts. The objective is to drum up good feelings about the drug firms among investors. So, do subtle pressures from public and private investment markets affect decisions related to drug company-sponsored clinical trials? Researchers at MIT, Harvard, and the University of Pennsylvania have studied this question, especially the central issue of whether firms rush through the early clinical trials of safety and efficacy while ignoring equivocal findings to satisfy holders of the purse strings and show sufficient progress to warrant future investments.[19]

Investigators were particularly interested in whether the larger, more financially secure firms, such as the integrated pharmaceutical companies, made wiser decisions to proceed or discontinue work on drug candidates at earlier stages of clinical development than did startup biopharmaceutical companies with comparatively shaky finances. The researchers confirmed these inferences—namely, that larger firms seemed to make better decisions earlier in the process.

The bottom line is this: Everyone knows drug development is costly and continuing to rise. This is due to all the reasons we've just discussed, but also because that "low-hanging fruit" has largely been picked. In other words, medicines for diseases that work in ways we understand—hypertension is a good example—have already been developed. Yes, improvements can be made, but increasingly drug companies find they must look for drugs that, for various reasons, have a smaller effect. The drugs work on fewer patients, either because of genetic differences among patients or because the pool of patients for these diseases is smaller. This has repercussions for clinical trials, too, because you need more patients to show the effects, and the more patients the more expensive the trial—hence the higher the development cost. But clinical trials are not the only part of the system in which business considerations are trumping science.

For much of the post–World War II period, the most influential decision makers in a pharmaceutical company were from the science side of the firm. Scientists would decide whether to initiate, proceed with, or discontinue development of a drug candidate. But as the revenue streams from early blockbusters began to face the threat of impending patent expirations, things changed. A new trend toward efficiency emerged, accelerated by the onset of managed care—perceived as a further threat to the revenue stream—and spurred by the continuing cry over ever-increasing drug prices and the access problems these high prices created. The firms in the industry answered with an internal reorganization. Looking to thwart the threats, the major pharmaceutical companies looked at how other industries operated and followed their example. They saw aerospace firms, for instance, managing their R & D more efficiently through a team approach.

*Today, the decisions once made by scientists well in advance of clinical trials are now made by multidisciplinary teams that include people from the business side of the company. Business considerations are now discussed hand in hand with the scientific issues at the earliest stages of pharmaceutical research.*

Today, the decisions once made by scientists well in advance of clinical trials are now made by multidisciplinary teams that include people from the business side of the company. Sometimes called "brand teams," they comprise scientists, clinicians, business development staff, and marketing staff, and they guide the process from the early scientific work through clinical testing to strategizing for market introduction and finally into post-marketing studies. In other words, business considerations are now discussed hand in hand with the scientific issues at the *earliest* stages of pharmaceutical research.

## *Where Are the Incentives to Meet Society's Needs?*

The third essential component for developing innovative drugs is incentives. To ensure that drug development is aligned with societal needs, incentives should reflect that objective. This may seem to suggest *mandating* the type of research that is done, but that is not our approach. Look at the successes the big pharmaceutical firms have enjoyed with blockbusters: Some of it came from the alignment of their drug-development programs with broad medical needs in society and the existence of a potential market within which to sell the new products profitably. Antidepressants, medicines for treating high blood pressure, and cholesterol-lowering drugs are all examples where pharmaceutical companies filled unmet medical needs for maintenance of chronic illnesses with big markets and the promise that many patients would need to take drugs every day for the rest of their lives. Surely we can create similar incentives when the market may not be blockbuster size but where society's need is great.

Unfortunately today, with rising costs in a broken system that sanctions putting business interests before science, those incentives are largely missing. Drug companies are in a tough spot: they're not charities, they have fiduciary responsibilities, and yet they make products that should be accessible to every person in the world who needs them. One brief story is enlightening. An executive at a major pharmaceutical firm was asked by his CEO to gauge whether a hunch he had was true: that every time the company made a contribution of medicines to a less-developed country, the firm's stock price went down. The answer doesn't really matter; it so happens that no direct correlation could be shown. What's disturbing is that the CEO asked the question at all!

Another example of skewed incentives is far more compelling and involves the issue of drug combinations. For a long time, the FDA was generally opposed to the idea of combining multiple drugs in, say, one capsule, because the regulators believed that limiting prescriptions to *individual* drugs made it easier to gauge therapeutic effects and isolate toxicity problems—overall, to keep things clean. But lately, the FDA's stance seems to have changed and the agency has become an advocate of combinations, which offer many potential benefits. For example, a patient who needs to take two drugs is much more likely to comply if she can take them in one capsule, once a day.

In the developing world, the stakes are even higher.[20] One of the challenges in dealing with the AIDS epidemic in Africa is that treatment requires a "cocktail" of drugs. In wealthier countries, patients are put on multiple drugs and then monitored closely for the impact on the amount of the virus in the bloodstream and the development of any resistance. But in Africa, the healthcare infrastructure for such monitoring is scarce. The position of aid agencies is almost unanimous: combine the drugs into one pill, give it to those who need it, and if some mistakes are made or resistances emerge, the overall benefit to African society is still a huge plus because at least most patients will get what they need.

The drugs that make up the cocktail, though, are made by different companies, which means alliances among manufacturers are needed to create a combination pill. But the incentives for alliances are largely nonexistent. What about patent protection to a company? A host of questions and concerns has slowed the combination of fixed doses of the AIDS cocktail for poor countries. However, now some generic manufacturers do make combination antivirals for sale in developing countries. And, finally, a joint venture between two firms to produce a three-drug combination antiviral, Atripia, is for sale in the U.S. market.

Usually, when combinations *do* happen, they are created for business reasons, not health and science reasons. Companies combine drugs as a way to extend their lines or to keep a dying product's patent protection intact with a minimally changed formulation. We need to create health incentives that align with the business incentives. We need incentives that, for instance, make combinations attractive to drug companies for the right reason—people's health—and that discourage rejecting the idea because of business considerations.

The idea of realigning incentives is not ours alone. In *Strong Medicine,* Michael Kremer and Rachel Glennerster point to many of the same problems we're describing. They focus on the need for vaccines in the less-developed world and examine why pharmaceutical researchers largely ignore the development of medicines for diseases that primarily affect low-income countries. Their conclusions, in a nutshell, reflect the same points we make about aligning incentives with societal needs: market size is a critical determinant of innovation; business decisions are being made rather than addressing medical needs (firms "fear they would not be able to sell . . . at prices that would cover their risk-adjusted costs"); and there need to be real, market-based incentives to make a shift.[21]

A shining new example could be a positive harbinger for combinations in the future. Merck and Schering crafted a complex agreement that enabled them to combine two drugs, Zocor and Zetia, to create *Vytorin,* a cholesterol-lowering drug that treats both the food source as well as the genetic source of high cholesterol. If these two industry giants can get together, there may be hope that others will follow suit.

We need every possible pharmaceutical innovation with promise to make it to the market at a price affordable for the patients who

*We need every possible pharmaceutical innovation with promise to make it to the market at a price affordable for the patients who need the drug.*

need the drug. We need drug development that focuses on the therapeutic value of drugs and not the business side of the equation. That can be accomplished only if we make sure that there are suitable monetary incentives in place, without the drug firms having to put sales and marketing ahead of scientific considerations. We contend that the pharmaceutical industry can still thrive, even if it concentrates on meeting medical needs—including in developing countries—instead of on market size. But it requires a fundamental reshaping of drug business.

The misalignment of incentives embodies much of what is broken about the system. We've shown you business people repeatedly making decisions that don't seem to have society's best interests in mind, but that nevertheless correspond exactly to what the system allows and even encourages. These are not bad people making bad decisions; they are people playing their roles according to the opportunities, constraints, and obligations of a system that has made the misalignment of incentives all too acceptable. As a society, we continue to pay for this misalignment in the form of high drug prices, limited access, and now reduced output of innovative medications.

Even if we could be sure that everyone concerned had the best of intentions, it's impossible to imagine a fix that doesn't attack the problem at a systemic level. Under the present industry structure, innovation and high prices go hand in hand. It's time to break that connection, and make it possible for innovation to continue while lowering drug prices—and ensure the future health of a vibrant pharmaceutical industry in the process. We believe we've found the solution: Change the way science and business interact in drug discovery and development.

# *Endnotes*

[1] PhRMA. 2006. R & D investments by America's pharmaceutical research companies near record $40 billion in 2005. Press release, February 13. For accounts of difference in calculating R & D expenditures, see Austin, David H. 2006. *Research and Development in the Pharmaceutical Industry*. Congress of the United States, Congressional Budget Office, October:7–8. See also: Public Citizen. 2001. Rebuttals to PhRMA responses to the Public Citizen Report, "Rx R & D myths: The case against the drug industry's R & D 'scare card.'" www.citizen.org/congress/reform/drug_industry/articles.cfm?ID=6514 (accessed April 23, 2007).

[2] Amarenco, P., J. Bogousslavsky, *et al.*, 2006. High-dose atorvastatin after stroke or transient ischemic attack. *New England Journal of Medicine* 255:6, 549–59.

[3] Bollier, D., S. Weiss, and K. O. Hanson. 1991. Merck and Co., Inc: Addressing third-world needs (A)—case study. Cambridge, Mass.: Harvard Business School Publishing.

[4] *Ibid.*

[5] Some drug companies have taken a different approach, "flat-pricing" their drugs. Since it costs about the same to produce a 20mg pill as a 10mg pill, the company charges the same for both doses. They have been burned, though, when HMOs began to distribute pill splitters to their patients, thus cutting the cost of the drug in half.

[6] The pending Fair Access to Clinical Trials Act, introduced in Congress in 2005, would mandate a broad expansion of how much information from clinical trials is made public. The information would be posted on a website, www.clinicaltrials.gov.

[7] Tufts Center for the Study of Drug Development. 2006. Average cost to develop a new biotechnology product is $1.2 billion. November 9. http://csdd.tufts.edu/NewsEvents/NewsArticle.asp?newsid=69 (accessed April 23, 2007). See also: Tufts Center for the Study of Drug Development. 2003. Total cost to develop a new prescription drug, including cost of post-approval research, is $897 million. May 13. http://155.212.10.127/NewsEvents/RecentNews.asp?newsid=29 (accessed April 23, 2007).

[8] Grabowski, H., J. Vernon, and J. A. DiMasi. 2002. Returns on research and development for 1990s new drug introductions. *Pharmacoeconomics* 20:Suppl.3,11–29. See also: Myers, S. C. and C. D. Howe. 1997. A life-cycle financial model of pharmaceutical R & D. MIT Program on the Pharmaceutical Industry (POPI) Working Paper 41–97 (April).

[9] Temin, 1980, *op. cit.*, 88–119.

[10] Bodenheimer, T. 2000. Uneasy alliances: Clinical investigators and the pharmaceutical industry. *Health Policy Report* 342:20.

[11] Rettig, R. A. 2000. The industrialization of clinical research. *Health Affairs* 19:2, 129–146.

[12] Drews, J. 2003. Strategic trends in the drug industry. *Drug Discovery Today* 8:9, 411–420.

[13] We are not addressing the movement of clinical trials offshore, especially to the developing world. While this happens with increasing frequency, the share of trials done in the United States remains high.

[14] Getz, Kenneth A. 2006. Personal communication with the authors, updating Getz, K. A. 1999. AMCs rekindling clinical research partnerships with industry. *Centerwatch*.

[15] Eichenwald, K. and G. Kolata. 1999. Drug trials hide conflicts for doctors; and A doctor's drug studies turn into fraud. *New York Times*, May 16 and 17. See also: Bekelman, J. E., Y. Li, and C. P. Gross. 2003. Scope and impact of financial conflicts of interest in biomedical research: A systematic review. *Journal of the American Medical Association* 289:4.

[16] Kassirer, Jerome P. 2004. *On the Take: How Medicine's Complicity with Big Business Can Endanger Your Health*. New York: Oxford University Press.

[17] Drews, 2003, *op. cit.*

[18] Kolata, G. 1993. Halted at the market's door: How a $1 billion drug failed. *New York Times*, February 12.

[19] Nicholson, S., P. Danzon, and J. McCullough. 2002. Biotech-pharmaceutical alliances as a signal of asset and firm quality. National Bureau of Economic Research Working Paper No. 9007. See also: Guedj, I. and D. Scharfstein. 2004. Organizational scope and investment: Evidence from the drug development strategies and performance of biopharmaceutical firms. National Bureau of Economic Research Working Paper No. 10933. See also: Bekelman, Li, and Gross, 2003, *op. cit.* See also: Kassirer, 2004, *op. cit.*

[20] Turano, T. R. Moore, and J. Gran. 2003. FDA opens new office to handle "combination products." *Mondaq Business Briefing*, June 23.

[21] Kremer, Michael and Rachel Glennerster. 2004. *Strong Medicine: Creating Incentives for Pharmaceutical Research on Neglected Diseases*. Princeton, NJ: Princeton University Press.

# CHAPTER SEVEN

## HOW TO LOWER DRUG PRICES

*If we can really understand the problem, the answer
will come out of it, because the answer is not
separate from the problem.*

—Jiddu Krishnamurti

T he crisis is real. Drug prices are high and getting higher. For those
fortunate enough to have health insurance, prescription co-payments
are rising, too. Money—whether it has to do with spending it or
making it—is an obstacle to getting needed medicines.

Just as science and technology take us to the cusp of therapeutic breakthroughs as monumental as the introduction of antibiotics
and just as we seem poised to realize the promise of "personalized"
medicine that can be targeted to the patients for whom it will really
work, we find ourselves stuck with a broken system that is already
working *against* these advances.

Or are we truly stuck? Fatalists might believe that nothing can
be done, that the future is one of either growing prices and reduced
access or government intervention with price controls and thus an
end to innovation. We're optimistic, though, because we have a solution to the crisis. It involves shifting risk and reconfiguring how we
get drugs from the discovery process through the many steps to
market.

Discovering new drugs and bringing them to consumers is a process fraught with uncertainty. The pitfalls companies encounter as they search for new drugs are considerable, but the pharmaceutical industry has been quite adroit at finding ways to continue its long run of profitable success and maintaining its focus on developing new blockbuster products. Since the uncertainty at the level of the drug itself has not, over the past three decades, carried over to the company level, our top pharmaceutical companies have enjoyed impressive stability and a level of profitability long the envy of firms in other sectors.

Nevertheless, the risks at the level of the individual drug candidate are real. And the biggest risk is showing up more and more on the radar screen: finding no new drugs that can be marketed. The uncertainty of whether a drug will be a blockbuster or even profitable is another matter. Pfizer's problems in late 2006 with its drug candidate torcetrapib illustrate the differences. This example also highlights why the crisis must be resolved with a new system that breaks out of the blockbuster mentality.

As mentioned briefly in Chapter 1, "Drugs and Drug Prices," Pfizer's new drug was going to be the company's savior by offsetting a key patent expiration in 2011—that of Lipitor, one of the world's biggest-selling drugs. The new drug was to have been a combination tablet containing Lipitor and *torcetrapib*, which inhibits bad cholesterol and enhances good cholesterol, for the potential treatment of two causes of cardiovascular disease: atherosclerosis and hypercholesterolemia. Analysts predicted it would become a top-selling medicine in the cardiovascular market, which explains Pfizer's $1 billion investment in its development and the accelerated program to get it to market before the Lipitor patent expires. But in Phase III trials, many more patients died with the new drug than did those on the standard treatment, and there were higher rates of other heart problems. Pfizer was forced to cancel its efforts to develop its next blockbuster.

The torcetrapib story shows how close a company can come to success and still be exposed to drug discovery risk. Further, it amplifies the point we made earlier about biomarkers. Imagine if Pfizer had developed torcetrapib with biomarkers and marketed a test to determine the population for which the drug would likely work. To be sure, that would have meant a smaller market for the company, but society would have something it doesn't have today—an effective drug for these particular patients with cardiovascular disease. Instead, society has nothing to show from this effort, and the failure of Pfizer's new drug in Phase III trials was a large enough shock to cause the company's stock to fall by 10 percent[1]—a loss of some $20 billion in market capitalization.[2] Since then, Pfizer has announced a 10 percent cut in its global workforce, and—perhaps most notably—the company's CEO has acknowledged implicitly that the company needs to "wean Pfizer from its blockbuster culture," as one analyst put it.[3] These two kinds of risks—the risk of failing to find a new drug and the chance that a new drug may not be very profitable—are linked together in the current industry structure. Companies that succeed in marketing have lots of capital with which to fund the research and development of their next new drugs. When prices are controlled, as in many countries, the chances of profiting tremendously from a blockbuster drug are all but eliminated, and companies simply don't do much drug research.

Financing R & D from pharmaceutical sales revenues has worked well in the United States for half a century. The high prices paid for drugs here have funded fruitful searches for new drugs ever since the discovery of effective antibiotics. But that arrangement is running into trouble. While drug *prices* continue to rise at a rapid rate, the rate of new drug *discovery* has been falling. It is a sign of the dysfunction in a broken system. And as the problems worsen, it leads pharmaceutical companies into the kinds of questionable practices we've already described—and the kinds of bad outcomes those practices can produce.

# Eliminate the Link between Drug Discovery and Prices

What's our solution to the drug-pricing problem? Eliminate the linkage between drug prices and drug discovery. Society desperately needs to limit the unfettered growth in drug prices so it can solve the pressing problem of access to needed medications. By eliminating the linkage, we can limit drug prices without fear of killing the research geese that lay golden eggs—namely, pills. We don't need to eliminate the uncertainty in the process of discovering new drugs; we have no more of an idea how to do that than any of the eminent scientists grappling with the issue every day. But by separating the risks of drug discovery and development from the chances inherent in marketing medicines, we can cut the Gordian knot that ties together high drug prices and the promise of new drugs.

Our solution does not specifically address the role of the FDA. While we encourage reforms of the mandate and the role of the FDA that can correct the agency's well-documented problems, that is a topic for a different discussion. Nor does our solution address how drugs are *found*. We have no magic formula or superior technology for predicting which putative drugs will emerge as useful; most likely, the processes will continue as they are today, changing with scientific and technological advances. For us, the key challenge to overcome in fixing the current broken system is to determine who will bear the risk. In the current system, drug companies absorb the risk and expect to be paid for their efforts and risk taking. By distributing the risk among several parties and groups, we can create a system—with the proper incentives—that turns a broken system into a working system.

The concept is simple. It begins with keeping the current drug development and production infrastructure intact, with drug development guided primarily by market incentives. In fact, incentives for drug discovery and development are preserved and even increased by having a new, independent, public, nonprofit Drug Development Corporation (DDC). Modeled after the best aspects of public-private partnerships of the past, when the government supported research and development initiatives for projects that were unsustainable by the private sector alone, the DDC would act as the intermediary to acquire new drugs that emerge from private- or public-sector R & D, then transfer the rights to sell the drugs to a different set of firms. Specifically, the DDC would pay a drug's developer for its patents. (In a section following this chapter, we provide details on every aspect of the solution described here.)

These payments to R & D firms would be large enough to offer a fair return for the money already spent on research and also provide incentives to continue to develop more new drugs. Then, the DDC would hold auctions to sell exclusive licenses to the qualified, highest-bidding companies with drug marketing expertise and a sales force. These firms would be subject to a cap on the price they could charge consumers for the drugs, and would have the opportunity to generate reasonable returns over what they paid at auction, plus marketing and distribution expenses.

## *Finance Drug Discovery with Savings from Lower Prices*

The financial resources for purchasing patents from discoverers would come from the federal government, which would be able to finance the process largely from the savings it would realize in many programs (such as Medicare Part D) from lower drug prices. And resources could also come from other sources: foundations, charities, and even foreign governments willing to make investments in drug development. R & D firms would receive larger payments for innovative drugs that fulfill unmet medical or public health needs, but lesser amounts for what might be new entrants in already crowded medicine classes. The more innovative or needed new drugs will bring higher prices at the auctions than would other drugs. But even the less attractive drugs should generate bidders at the auction, so long as the marketplace provides an opportunity to generate reasonable revenues and profits.

Production and distribution of drugs, which entail only low-to-moderate risks, can remain private. However, with our solution, the public must and will assume a large share of the high financial risks of scientific discovery and clinical testing. And the DDC can set new priorities for deciding which drugs to develop so that "unmet medical needs" and underserved populations are addressed. Further, to safeguard society's interests in scientific advances, the DDC could even consider buying the patents of technological breakthroughs that may facilitate future drug discovery, to ensure that restrictions on the use of knowledge never become impediments to finding the medicines we need.

How would this work in practice? Consider the example of Merck's new vaccine against the *human papillomavirus*, which is responsible for 70 percent of observed cases of cervical cancer. Many health officials advocate that this vaccine be administered essentially to all adolescent girls before they become sexually active. The size of that target population in the United States alone would approach 20 million people.[4] Today, Merck—which sells its own products—has priced the vaccine at more than $300 for the three-injection series.

With our solution, a marketing firm unconnected to Merck would have bid for and won the rights to sell the vaccine. Because this product potentially has an impact on a critical health concern and could prevent millions of cases of a sometimes fatal disease, the DDC would be expected to pay the vaccine's developer a hefty sum, well in excess of what it would be expected to receive at auction when it sells the marketing rights. The marketing firm that wins the auction would be subject to a maximum selling price for the vaccine of, say, $75 for the three-shot series, closer to the expected price of a seasonal flu vaccine.

Although the concept of separating drug development from sales and marketing is simple, we do have to admit up front that ours is a *radical* solution. But what makes it radical is precisely why it's so necessary today: It puts the good of society front and center, while at the same time maintains the spirit of free enterprise that has been the engine of innovation in the United States. In the case of an effective cervical cancer vaccine, everyone wins, including society at large, which avoids the high direct and indirect costs associated with rampant cervical cancer among the population.

> *Our solution puts the good of society front and center, while at the same time maintaining the spirit of free enterprise that has been the engine of innovation in the United States.*

## Undo the Blockbuster Mentality

Our solution is at once a rejection of the kind of price controls that have handcuffed pharmaceutical innovation in other countries and an embrace of a fundamental reality that our system is broken. By eliminating the linkage between drug prices and drug discovery, we can undo the blockbuster mentality that is no longer a fitting model for the business side of the pharmaceutical industry.

What is gained from the new system? Why insert the government as a funder and policymaker into what has been a private activity for so long? What, more specifically, are the advantages of separating drug discovery and marketing?

The first advantage is to eradicate the kinds of abuses we chronicled in earlier chapters. Our solution immediately eliminates many of the perverse incentives that exist today as a direct result of the linkage. No longer will those who *discover* drugs be tied directly to those who seek to generate ever higher revenues from drug sales, which means that researchers can concentrate on what society needs and marketers can figure out how to generate revenue. Incentives in our new system will be more closely aligned with the general welfare.

Second, our solution corrects what is perhaps the *most* perverse aspect of the current, broken system: Sick people are the ones who pay for drug discovery. The high prices they or their insurers pay fund the discovery of the next generation of drugs. By providing resources for drug discovery differently, the general population—including healthy people—will pay for the research and development of new drugs. Healthy people tend to be working, while sick people often cannot work. Healthy taxpayers also tend to be at the peak of their earning capability, while sick people are often old and retired. And, of course, the number of healthy people in America far outstrips the number of those who are sick. Isn't it better that everyone shares in the financing of drug discovery rather than try to extract the resources out of people who are already ill?

Third, correcting the perverse funding mechanism just described will alleviate emerging problems in our current jumble of health-insurance provisions. Drugs are only a small part of health-care insurance; in fact, they were omitted entirely from Medicare at its formation 40 years ago. As drug prices have risen, however, the demand for prescription drug benefits as part of health insurance has grown. The government's Medicare Part D is both wildly expensive and poor insurance, as we showed in Chapter 5, "How *Not* to Lower Drug Prices." Written in large part by the big pharmaceutical companies, the law keeps alive the research geese that lay golden eggs (pills) by paying their owners the difference between the consumers' price of drugs and the manufacturers' cost of producing them. If we want low prices and new drugs, it is simpler for the government to pay for research directly than to subsidize Big Pharma, the largest pharmaceutical companies, in the hopes it will continue to produce the new medicines we need.

## Develop the Drugs Society Truly Needs

Our solution would correct the current imbalance between the development of drugs that are of greatest value to society and those that can simply bring in the most profit. So-called "me-too" drugs, for instance, usually have commercial value well in excess of their social value. Drugs for tropical diseases are a primary case of drugs undervalued by the American market. Our current broken system has established incentives that are just plain wrong for determining which drugs a developer ought to pursue.

> *Our solution would correct the current imbalance between the development of drugs that are of greatest value to society and those that can simply bring in the most profit.*

Here's a case in point. Developing countries with tropical and subtropical climates desperately need a vaccine against malaria (which, with global warming, is an increasing threat to other parts of the world, too). In *Strong Medicine*, Michael Kremer and Rachel Glennerster describe failed efforts by the United States Agency for International Development (USAID) to stimulate development of a drug to prevent malaria.[5] A suitable incentive would be an advance commitment from governments of wealthy countries to purchase large numbers of such a vaccine once developed. With our solution to the problem, the DDC would pay a generous sum to the vaccine's developers, and it then would accept a low auction price for the selling rights due to the small size of the paying market for the product. As long as firms could make a financial return in line with the costs and risks they would assume, we would expect them to show interest in bidding.

How would our solution be implemented? It begins with the "de-integration" of all existing pharmaceutical firms, in a manner analogous to the changes that took place in the telecommunications and electric power industries late in the twentieth century.[6] In other words, the major drug companies must divest their R & D functions. To enforce this divestiture, the FDA would be ordered not to accept NDAs (New Drug Applications) from firms that continue to market drugs. The work of drug development is too important to society to let it continue to unfold in a framework of decision-making based on a broken system with flawed incentives.

Once the divestiture of R & D is complete, a reorganized pharmaceutical industry would be comprised of firms that engage either in drug discovery and development or that are manufacturing and distribution companies. Today's large, integrated pharmaceutical firms would become separate firms in each of these two sectors. Many smaller biopharmaceutical firms would continue unchanged as contributors to the new R & D sector. Existing generic companies would be largely unchanged within the new manufacturing and distribution sector. And the FDA would be barred from dealing with new drug discoveries by firms that it deals with on the marketing side.

## Change the Incentives

How does this change the incentives to do drug development that best serves society? The federal government would create the DDC to be an interface between the new discovery/development and manufacturing/distribution sectors and to represent society's best interests. Its independence from the government must be assured, so that its decisions are insulated from political considerations (such as controversies over the funding of embryonic stem cell research) that could interfere with scientific progress.

Funding of the DDC would be through public funds, but philanthropic contributions and even contributions from foreign governments would be welcome. Its main funding, though, would come from the set of auctions it would run. It is through these auctions that firms in the marketing/distribution sector would acquire new drugs from the discovery/development firms. The best aspects of the auctions used today for wireless telecommunications licenses offer a beginning model. Drug licenses would be sold at auction only to private companies, to make the auction serious. And drug developers would be paid from the money received from the auctions.

The payment for a drug, though, would not be determined solely by the auction price. It typically would exceed the eventual auction price because the payment may be increased according to the value placed on that particular type of drug by the DDC. The DDC would set priorities for new drugs based on impartial, objective assessments of medical and societal needs not only in the industrialized countries, taking into account indigent, middle class, and wealthy populations, but also in the developing world. And *science* would rule the decision-making. We expect that most payments to discovering firms would be larger than the winning bid.

Putting science ahead of business considerations is key to our solution. The announcement of *ASAQ*, a new treatment for malaria introduced in March 2007, is the kind of news we would expect to see much more of with our solution. The drug combines *artemisin*, a Chinese invention that uses sweet wormwood, with an older anti-malaria drug called *amodiaquine*. The new combination is relatively inexpensive—less than $1 a day for adults and less than 50 cents for children—and will even come in one-a-day sizes for infants, which is a first. A major pharmaceutical company, Sanofi-Aventis, teamed with the Drugs for Neglected Diseases Initiative, a project of the international charity *Médecins Sans Frontières*, to produce the medicine.[7]

It is possible to set priorities based on science, and even to ensure that the process is not

> *It is possible to set priorities based on science, and even to ensure that the process is not influenced by special interests or the politics of the moment.*

influenced by special interests or the politics of the moment. A straightforward two-stage review, like the process the NIH uses to determine distribution of its research funds, can involve specialists in the natural and social sciences and medicine with experience in drug development and health care. The NIH has managed, for more than half a century, to distribute funding according to scientific merit, with minimal interference by special interests.

The first stage of the review by a multidisciplinary group of experts would address the technical tasks of setting priorities for drug development and determining the value that should be added to auction prices. In a second stage, advisory panels populated by recognized thought leaders broadly representative of society would be charged with determining whether the recommendations of the first-stage reviewers should be endorsed. (In the Appendix following this chapter that details our solution, we suggest that expert panels constituted, for example, by the United States Pharmacopeia and the National Academy of Sciences could manage, respectively, the first and second stages of the review.) This review process would be so much better than leaving the decisions in the hands of marketers.

Don't confuse our solution with a government takeover of the pharmaceutical industry. The new discovery/development industry sector would accommodate all types of current players in pharmaceutical R & D—the divested research arms of major drug firms, small biopharmaceutical firms, clinical trials contract research organizations, and hybrids of these. Firms could continue to be financed, as is now the case, through venture capital, other private investors, or the public markets. Universities and nonprofit research institutes would be encouraged to become further engaged in the process of discovering and developing drugs. All such organizations would have access to federal grants made available through the NIH. They could form collaborations and alliances with other players in the sector, collaborations that have been shown to be consistent with greater R & D productivity. They would be able to take full advantage of economies of scale that have been shown to benefit the discovery/development process.[8]

One of the big changes where science would clearly be put ahead of business would be in the dissemination of information. The results of all basic scientific studies and clinical trials would be submitted for publication in peer-reviewed journals as soon as patent and other intellectual property considerations permit. Should a study produce "negative" results deemed insufficiently significant for publication in major journals, those results would still be made available as public record by the DDC.

## *Prices Will be Lower*

How will prices be lowered? The DDC will conduct auctions to license newly discovered drug candidates after Phase III trials are complete. Firms in the manufacturing/distribution sector can then bid competitively. The terms of the drug licenses will include a maximum price at which the new drug can be offered in the U.S. marketplace, set in relation to the costs of manufacturing and competitively marketing new drugs. The firms in this sector assume the *moderate* risks of manufacturing and distribution, but not the *higher* risks of discovery and development, and their return will be in line accordingly. After the patents on the new drugs have expired, the entry of generics will drive prices even lower.

The marketing firms would do so-called *Phase IV testing*, which will be the post-launch safety surveillance. If they find more indications for drugs they're marketing, these firms will benefit. If adverse effects emerge, the marketing firm bears these risks as well, as in today's system. And, to avoid any conflict of interest, these firms marketing drugs will have to work with different testing companies than do the firms working on discovery and development.

Many of the functions associated with drug R & D or production are currently carried out by affiliated firms through arrangements that include subcontracting, licensing, or alliances, as described earlier. The current, large pharmaceutical firms license some drug candidates from small biopharmaceutical firms, while developing others in-house. Those same large firms often opt to hire a CRO (Contract Research Organization) to oversee various aspects of their clinical testing, also described earlier. And many different types of firms, including both large R & D-based drug firms and generic firms, competently perform manufacturing, especially of small molecule drugs (chemical drugs). The infrastructure that currently exists to carry out the full spectrum of activities to bring a drug from research to market could continue to operate in much the same way as it does today.

The discovery risk—that a molecule won't make it to market (detailed earlier)—will not be borne by the drug distribution firms. These companies will have obtained their drugs through auction, and won't need to or even be able to justify high drug prices on the basis of the high cost of discovering drugs. The auctions will be for the 13 percent of drugs actually approved by the FDA after surviving development and testing. Today, patent protection *allows* companies to charge high prices, with the high cost of development providing the *justification*. Our solution takes this justification off the table. Prices will be limited by the terms of patent licenses.

## Reduce the Staggering Cost of Capital

One way our solution realigns incentives with society's needs is by reducing the risk to firms in the drug discovery/development sector. Since their successful drugs will be sold at auction after the FDA approves them, drug discoverers will be paid sooner than they are today, when revenues come in over the patent life of the drug. This reduces the length of time they must bear their risk, and hence reduces the cost of capital (the rate of return that could be earned in the capital market on securities of equivalent risk), which is staggering in the pharmaceutical industry.

Our solution also makes the work of advocacy groups for patients with particular diseases or classes of disease more viable. New drug development companies could form as nonprofits willing to absorb risk because of their mission. Particular groups or foundations interested in certain diseases may be willing to bear the risk of drug development in areas that interest them.[9] Non-governmental organizations devoted to the search for cures, such as those described in the "Putting Finding the Cure Ahead of Profits" accompanying box, will find it encouraging to deal with the DDC and will be able to help society in a new, potentially more valuable way.

## PUTTING FINDING THE CURE AHEAD OF PROFITS

Our broken system for getting drugs from the laboratory to the patients who need them has spurred all sorts of nonprofit, non-governmental initiatives. The two described below illustrate the pressing need to realign the business incentives of the pharmaceutical industry with society's needs.

The *Institute for OneWorld Health*, which identifies itself as a "non-profit pharmaceutical company," was founded in 2000 to develop anti-infective drugs and vaccines for diseases prevalent in the developing world that kill millions of people each year. New drugs for these diseases rarely reach the market,[10] and those that do typically cost far in excess of what any of the patients can afford to pay. So, OneWorld Health solicits donations of potential drug candidates from for-profit pharmaceutical companies and academic researchers and develops them into safe and effective medicines. These efforts are funded by private groups, governments, and—in particular—the Bill and Melinda Gates Foundation. OneWorld Health then joins with companies, hospitals, and organizations in the target countries to evaluate the new drug, eventually transferring the patent rights to manufacture and supply the medicine at reasonable prices.[11] Successes thus far include a cure for the deadly parasitic disease known as *black fever* that kills half a million people each year and threatens 350 million people in 88 countries.[12]

*FasterCures* (its formal name is the Center for Accelerating Medical Solutions, or CAMS), is a self-described "action-tank" based in Washington, D.C., that focuses on overcoming the inefficiencies in research into Alzheimer's, epilepsy, prostate cancer, juvenile diabetes, and breast cancer.[13] It was founded in 2003 by Michael Milken. Unlike OneWorld Health, FasterCures does no drug development itself. Rather, the center brings together multidisciplinary groups to assess the process of scientific and clinical research and create policy solutions by removing obstacles and adjusting process priorities. Its efforts often focus on changing tax policies to promote research, working to remove inefficiencies in the grant process, and supporting patient involvement in clinical trials. It is an extension of Milken's Prostate Cancer Foundation, established in 1993 to "stimulate research by drastically cutting the wait time for grant money, to flood the field with fast cash," and generally push the envelope to ensure greater collaboration, quicker results, and more outside-the-box thinking.

Under our plan, drug discovery may be part of a joint process to produce a variety of products, such as basic research and education. Failures can become public opportunities to transfer the knowledge generated and build on that knowledge, rather than just combining the costs of failure and passing it on to consumers in the form of higher prices (as happens today) or sinking an entire enterprise. Our solution distributes risk in another way, too. Many firms engaged in drug research and discovery fail, and the costs of their failure are borne by their investors as well as society in general through the bankruptcy laws. Our solution spreads this risk even more generally through society, rather than leaving it concentrated among the sick.

Treatments for maladies that today are ignored or never show up on the radar screen could get a new lease on life with our solution. Take *acute renal failure (ARF)*, for which there is no sure-fire treatment. It's also more prevalent than statistics reflect, because ARF often afflicts people when they're already in the hospital for something else, and the focus in "official" reporting captures what they were admitted for more accurately than what might have happened subsequently. This absence of accurate statistics keeps it off the radar screens of drug developers.

In the years before firms figured out that they could successfully charge extraordinarily high prices for certain small-market, high-impact medications, a major drug company discovered some compounds that offered promise in treating ARF. Business decisions, though, essentially put the drug to death before it could ever help a patient. Because the "official" reporting of incidences of ARF made the market look small, it was hard to justify the investment in development—especially considering the financial risk. Later, one of the authors was part of a group that visited the company in an effort to convince the business people to revive the program. The group argued that developing the compound and potentially marketing a drug for acute renal failure was supported by the fact that the firm could likely justify charging a high price. After all, the treatment would avert hospital-related costs for patients taking the medication. That argument won the day, and the scientists continued their work—although, unfortunately, the ARF drug later was found to be too toxic for humans.

## *Why Use an Independent Drug Development Corporation?*

Our solution changes radically the manner in which drug discovery and development are financed. The nonprofit, independent Drug Development Corporation would be at the center, the interface between public and private markets and the public interest facilitating co-investment by government and private firms to increase the share of drug development financed by the public.

Why an independent corporation model? The DDC would operate in the marketplace with the flexibility of a private-sector organization but completely accountable to public oversight. That's the best way to ensure a continued steady stream of innovations in pre-scription pharmaceuticals while lowering prices and ensuring access for all who need drugs.

This would not be the first time the federal government has established an independent, nonprofit corporation. In 1938, the Federal National Mortgage Association—known as "Fannie Mae"—was created to encourage lenders to invest in Federal Housing Authority (FHA) mortgages. Effectively a nationwide savings and loan institution, Fannie Mae made it possible for low- and middle-income households to afford down payments and monthly mortgage payments. In 1970, Fannie Mae was converted to a government-sponsored private enterprise and an additional entity, Federal Home Loan and Mortgage Company ("Freddie Mac"), was added to the mix. That same year, the federal government addressed a crisis in the nation's post office by creating the U.S. Postal Service, separating postal operations from the government—the postmaster general had been a member of the president's cabinet—as a nonprofit corporation.

Twenty years later, in an effort much closer to the aim of the DDC, the government began to use private, nonprofit corporations to stimulate innovation. The roots of this effort go back to the mid-twentieth century, when the government began to support private research and development initiatives in several areas to maintain social returns on innovation. As the Cold War was winding down, the government "began to put even more emphasis on research leading to commercially viable outcomes."[14] In 1987, U.S.–based semiconductor manufacturers and the U.S. government formed SEMATECH to leverage resources and share risks in a bold effort to strengthen the U.S. semiconductor industry. The government formed the Advanced Technology Program as a private corporation with public funding to invest in promising technologies, in the same way that Fannie Mae invested in mortgages. President George H. W. Bush's 1990 U.S. Technology Policy used federal funding for social improvement.[15]

The organizational structure we recommend for the DDC—an independent, public, nonprofit corporation—draws certain characteristics from the setup of the U.S. Postal Service and others from the Independent System Operators (ISOs) that today manage the interface between electric power generation and distribution. These ISOs are responsible for ensuring reliability and establishing and overseeing competitive wholesale electricity markets, serving the interests of providers, consumers, and society as a whole—much like the DDC's mandate.

## *Funding Our Solution*

Of course, our solution will require some legislative action. And at first glance, it would appear that making our solution operational is going to cost a lot of money. After all, the government would need to assume a major part, perhaps the lion's share, of funding of drug development—around $30 billion annually, as discussed earlier. But with either of the two scenarios that would emerge, a substantial portion of this money—even as much as 100 percent—could come from the savings realized as a result of fixing the broken system.

First, some of the funding would be offset by the lower prices the government would pay for drugs as part of Medicare, Medicaid, and the Veterans Administration (VA) and Department of Defense (DOD) healthcare systems. We believe that drug prices could drop by half if our solution is implemented, which would fund two-thirds of the $30 billion in drug R & D costs just from Medicare savings (see the "Medicare Part D Savings Alone Could Fund Our Solution" sidebar). Also, there would be substantial savings in the costs associated with price negotiations and economic evaluations of the use of medicines. But even if drug prices fell by less than half, the savings could be put back into funding the DDC.

## MEDICARE PART D SAVINGS ALONE COULD FUND OUR SOLUTION

Suppose drug prices fall by at least half, as we suspect they will if our solution is implemented. Let's look at what that would mean for the cost we're all bearing for Medicare Part D, and how that could fund the DDC's work. Here's a "back of the envelope" calculation.

First, as described in Chapter 5, let's start with the initial predicted cost of the Medicare drug benefit, put at $400 billion over 10 years or $40 billion per year. Further, let's anticipate that the rate of roughly 20 new chemical entities the FDA approves each year as new drugs remains constant. Add to the mix the cost of developing a new drug, for which R & D firms should be compensated; that's been estimated at around $1 billion (including capital costs and risks that will not be borne by the DDC, but we'll use the figure nonetheless).

If the DDC compensates 20 drug discoverers at this rate of $1 billion per new drug, then the cost of our solution will be half the cost of Medicare Part D. In this case, the DDC's activities could be financed largely by savings from Medicare Part D. This hypothetical cost is two-thirds of the total estimated current size of pharmaceutical R & D of $30 billion. If Medicare Part D is more expensive, as seems likely, saving half its cost will come close to financing all of our anticipated drug discovery and development. Savings from the VA and other programs also will add to the DDC's resources. With lower drug prices, government will be able to transfer funds from support of the current pharmaceutical industry to support of drug R & D.

The drug benefit in Medicare Part D will become cheaper as drug prices go down, as will the costs of other government programs such as those implemented by the VA. And as drug prices decline and the government's costs fall, resources will be freed up for direct support of drug discovery. The DDC will not need to wait for the savings in Medicare Part D and other drug programs to be realized since it can predict the savings from the terms of its drug licenses. Instead, the two processes of financing new drugs and saving on government drug insurance will unfold at the same time.

Suppose the rate of drug discovery improves. While we don't expect this to happen, it would increase DDC costs as they pay for more drug development. But that's hardly a problem for at least two reasons. It is possible that total government payments for drugs will fall even if the number of new drugs increases. And if the rate of drug discovery accelerates, perhaps because new incentives are drawing more scientists with good ideas to the field, we believe everyone would be quite happy and regard whatever extra DDC expenses result as a worthwhile expenditure for our nation—and perhaps our world—to improve health.

## The Time to Act Is Now

The benefits of our solution go well beyond fixing a broken system of high prices and out-of-kilter incentives. We expect to see improved output, with all sorts of innovative new products emerging from wider scientific explorations and a revitalized process. Participating firms will be in a much better position than they are today to take full advantage of the biological, chemical, and information technology revolutions that continue to unfold—without putting business considerations ahead of science and society's needs. Firms that today steer clear of developing orphan drugs and products for underserved populations will be attracted by the opportunity to capture large rewards offered for their work. Patients around the world will feel the benefits of new and improved therapies.

> *The benefits of our solution go well beyond fixing a broken system of high prices and out-of-kilter incentives. We expect to see improved output, with all sorts of innovative new products emerging from wider scientific explorations and a revitalized process.*

Equally important, drug prices will decrease and access to needed medicines will greatly improve. As prices of similar drugs fall within a narrow range and the costs of price negotiations plummet, the savings can be plowed directly into making the next big medical advances. And all of this will unfold in a climate of open scientific exchange that has always proved most conducive to progress. New and existing private- and public-sector R & D organizations will have every opportunity to take full advantage of economies of scale and engage in the kinds of scientific collaboration associated with the highest levels of R & D productivity.

The benefits of medical research have well exceeded the costs over time.[16] We agree with those who advocate for greater direct government funding of medical research through the NIH. Our solution will augment that kind of additional funding by establishing a mechanism for doing research that makes the best sense for society *and* makes sense for the bottom line.

Our patient—today's system—is not just broken, but is in critical condition. Affording access to modern medicines, while at the same time encouraging the continued development of new and innovative ones, is an absolute imperative for society. Changing how drug development is financed is the key to achieving these goals.

Others recognize the need for urgent action. The Medical Innovation Prize Act of 2005, first introduced in the House of Representatives by Bernie Sanders of Vermont (now a Senator), was being revised in the first months of 2007 for reintroduction. The bill is similar to our solution in some ways. It establishes a board of trustees similar to our DDC. It offers a "prize" to drug discoverers that is akin to the payments our solution would establish. So, while we commend the effort, Sanders' bill does not go far enough to address the problems we've described. It seems to set an arbitrary sum to be paid for newly discovered drugs; our payments would be set by auction, establishing transparency to reveal the value set by the market. And it has no procedure to vary payments for drug patents according to expert judgment regarding social needs and social benefits.

Still, the Sanders bill recognizes the essential point that the crisis will be resolved only if we *separate* the funding of drug research from the marketing of pharmaceuticals.

Look again at torcetrapib, which we discussed at the beginning of this chapter. The drug was supposed to succeed Lipitor as Pfizer's new blockbuster, which was prescribed 79 million times in 2005 for people in the United States alone.[17] But Pfizer abandoned its efforts to obtain FDA approval to market the new drug when clinical trials found it to be toxic; in comparison to Lipitor, the combination tablet was associated with a 60 percent increase in the mortality rate.[18] Because Pfizer was only interested in a blockbuster—a business strategy long supported by our broken system—the abandonment of torcetrapib means that those patients and tens of thousands of eventual users like them will be deprived of an innovative medicine that probably would have been effective in raising their levels of good blood cholesterol and, in turn, preventing heart disease.

With a functioning Drug Development Corporation, the R & D firm that developed the drug might have opted to identify a genetic marker (or some other kind of biomarker) to predict the people in whom the drug would be toxic, so they would never get a prescription. Those for whom the drug was safe could realize its benefits. And even though the size of the market for this new drug might be only, say, one-fourth of the market for Lipitor, it still would have brought an attractive payment from the DDC to the developing firm. Isn't it likely that at auction the opportunity to market the new drug along with its biomarker diagnostic test would have been an attractive business proposition to a number of prospective selling firms? We certainly think so. Large, traditional drug company marketing groups, as well as some of the firms that today specialize in marketing generic drugs, would embrace the chance to sell a product for a ready-made patient population. It makes good business sense and society wins, too.

Not fixing the broken system could be disastrous. If the pharmaceutical industry continues to operate with its blockbuster mentality, might the most profitable industry in the world be heading for a productivity crash? What will happen to innovation then? Or perhaps high prices will reach a tipping point and legislators will decide that price controls must be imposed. Direct price controls have killed innovation in most of the countries where they exist.

Neither alternative will achieve lower prices *and* continued innovation. The time to act is now, with a real solution for a new day.

## *Endnotes*

[1] Sinclair, A. 2006. Pfizer: Torcetrapib failure compounds current problems. *Pharmaceutical Business Review Online*, December 5.

[2] Berenson, A. and A. Pollack. 2006. Pfizer shares plummet on loss of a promising heart drug. *New York Times*, December 5.

[3] Nocera, J. 2007. The dangers of swinging for the fences. *New York Times*, January 27.

[4] Calculated from U.S. Census Bureau. 2000. Female population by age, race, and hispanic or Latino origin for the United States. www.census.gov/population/cen2000/phc-t9/tabo03.pdf (accessed April 24, 2007).

[5] Kremer and Glennerster, 2004, *op. cit.*

[6] Temin, Peter (with Louis Galambos). 1987. *The Fall of the Bell System: A Study in Prices and Politics*. New York: Cambridge University Press. See also: Joskow, Paul. 2000. Deregulation and regulatory reform in the U.S. electric power sector. In Peltzman, Sam and Clifford Winston. *Deregulation of Network Industries: The Next Steps*. Washington, D.C: Brookings Press.

[7] McNeil, Jr., D. G. 2007. Low-cost antimalaria pill available. *New York Times*, March 1.

[8] Cockburn, I. M. and R. M. Henderson. 2001. Scale and scope in drug development: Unpacking the advantages of size in pharmaceutical research. *Journal of Health Economics* 20:6, 1033–1057. See also: Henderson, R. M., and I. M. Cockburn. 1996. Scale, scope, and spillovers: The determinants of research productivity in drug discovery. *RAND Journal of Economics* 27:1, 32–59.

[9] The ALS Association. 2004. Update on stem cell research and potential treatments for ALS (August 6). www.alsa.org/research/article.cfm?id=455&CFID=40024&CFTOKEN=82131578 (accessed April 23, 2007). See also: www.michaeljfox.org/index.cfm.

[10] Trouiller, P., P. Olliaro, *et al.* 2002. Drug development for neglected diseases: A deficient market and a public-health policy failure. *The Lancet* 359: 2188.

[11] Case Western Reserve University, Weatherhead School of Management, Center for Business as an Agent of World Benefit. 2006. Profile of innovation—OneWorld Health: A new model for pharmaceutical industry. http://worldbenefit. cwru.edu/innovation/bankInnovationView.cfm?idArchive=368 (accessed April 23, 2007).

[12] Mandelbaum-Schmid, J. 2004. New generation of nonprofit initiatives tackles world's "neglected" diseases. *Bulletin of the World Health Organization* 84:5.

[13] Daniels, C., D. Burke, and P. Neering. 2004. The man who changed medicine. *Fortune* 150:11, 90–112.

[14] Stiglitz, J. E. and S. J. Wallsten. 1999. Public-private technology partnerships: Promises and pitfalls. *The American Behavioral Scientist* 43:1, 52.

[15] Link, A. N. and J. T. Scott. 2001. Public-private partnerships: Stimulating competition in a dynamic market. *International Journal of Industrial Organization* 19, 763–794.

[16] Cutler, David M. 2004. *Your Money or Your Life: Strong Medicine for America's Healthcare System*. New York: Oxford University Press.

[17] Henderson, D. 2006. Backed by study, Pfizer intensifies Lipitor pitch. *The Boston Globe*, September 5:E1.

[18] Sinclair, 2006, *op. cit.*

# APPENDIX

## OUR SOLUTION IN DETAIL

*If you've read Chapter 7, "How to Lower Drug Prices," the only reason to read this appendix is to learn how our plan to lower drug prices would work in detail. We've written this section primarily for policymakers and others we hope will be influenced by our arguments to take action and address the prescription drug crisis before it gets any worse.*

*The language here is the language of economics and policy, chosen with precision to facilitate the development of legislation. Chapter 7 presents our solution in lay terms.*

Our solution to the problem of high drug prices, outlined in Chapter 7, would change the *financing* of drug research and development and eliminate the linkage between drug prices and drug discovery—the underlying source of the current problem with high drug prices. This section details how our solution would work and discusses more of the rationale behind its conception.

Under our solution, all existing pharmaceutical firms would be "de-integrated" in a manner analogous to the changes that took place in the telecommunications and electric power industries late in the twentieth century.[1] Pharmaceutical companies would be divided into two parts, similar to the way the Bell System was divided in the 1980s and electric utilities were divided in the 1990s. Phrased differently, the major drug companies would divest their R & D functions. The results would be that firms in the reorganized pharmaceutical industry would be either drug discovery/development firms or manufacturing/distribution firms. Today's large, integrated pharmaceutical firms would evolve into separate firms in each of these two sectors. Many smaller biopharmaceutical firms would be unchanged and become contributors to the new R & D sector. Existing generic companies would be largely unchanged and serve as members of the new manufacturing and distribution sector.

The new discovery/development industry sector would accommodate all types of current players in pharmaceutical R & D—the divested research arms of major drug firms, small biopharmaceutical firms, contract research organizations (CROs), and hybrids of these. Firms could continue to be financed, as is now the case, through venture capital, other private investors, or the public markets. Universities and nonprofit research institutes would be encouraged to become further engaged in the process of discovery and developing drugs. All such organizations would have access to federal grants to be made available through the National Institutes of Health (NIH).

The federal government would create the independent, nonprofit Drug Development Corporation (DDC) to serve as the interface between the new discovery/development and manufacturing/distribution industry sectors. The DDC would be separate from the government to insulate its decisions from political considerations (such as controversies over the funding of embryonic stem cell research) that could interfere with scientific progress.

The DDC would receive proceeds from a set of auctions, modeled after telecommunications license auctions, through which drug marketing/distribution firms would acquire patent licenses for new drugs from the DDC after the Food and Drug Administration (FDA) has approved them. These licenses typically would include *price controls* for the sale of drugs—a maximum price at which the new drug could be offered in the U.S. marketplace. Discovery/development firms would provide complete patent portfolios for new drugs to the DDC earlier in exchange for payment after the auction. These firms would be paid from the results of the auctions, with a multiplier that could be more or less than 1 to reflect the priority for the type of new drug involved. The DDC would be financed with public funds in addition to the auction revenues in order to pay a multiplier for some drugs. Philanthropic contributions also would be welcomed, as would contributions from foreign governments.

Phase III trials would be concluded by the time the auctions take place and the marketing company would be responsible for Phase IV tests. To avoid conflicts of interest, testing companies would be prohibited from working for R & D firms and marketing firms at the same time.

Our solution would not eliminate the risks associated with drug discovery that we discussed in several earlier chapters. We believe these risks are inherent in the process of finding new drugs, and we take account of these risks in our solution.

Our solution also does not affect the process by which new drugs are found, only the way in which it is financed. We have no superior technology for predicting which putative drugs will emerge as useful; we anticipate that the industry will continue to be ruled by something like the current sequence of probabilities. The question, then, is who will bear the risk. In the current system, drug companies absorb this risk and expect to be paid for their efforts and risk-taking—thus, drugs are very expensive. Under our solution, these risks are shared among several parties and groups, which will result in lower prices.

The large risk of finding drug candidates that make it through to FDA approval will be spread among many firms engaged in drug research and discovery. Many of them will fail, as small firms do all the time. The cost of failure is borne by their investors as well as society in general through the bankruptcy laws. So here, too, the risks will be spread among a wide variety of people, not concentrated among the sick.

Several other factors reduce the risk to these firms. Since successful drugs, once approved by the FDA, will be sold to marketing firms, drug discoverers will be paid sooner than they are when the revenues come in over the patent life of the drug. This reduces the length of time risk must be borne and hence the cost of capital. Some of the drug-development companies may be nonprofits. If so, they will be working for reasons not dependent strictly on profits and they may be willing to absorb risk because of their mission. Particular groups or foundations interested in certain diseases may be willing to bear the risk of drug development in areas that interest them. In fact, some of these nonprofits may be parts of larger organizations with multiple purposes. Drug discovery may be part of a joint process to produce a variety of products, such as basic research and education. If so, failure to find a new drug may not be failure of the whole enterprise, but only a reduction in the success of one part of a multi-pronged process—or perhaps not even that if some aspect of the "failed" research proves useful for another purpose. Because the details of failures will be publicly disclosed, there will be wider opportunities to transfer the knowledge generated and to build on that knowledge.

Let's look more closely at the specific elements of our solution.

## *Establish a Nonprofit Drug Development Corporation*

Our solution to change radically the manner in which drug discovery and development are financed requires the establishment of an organization that acts as an interface between public and private markets and the public interest. We call this entity the Drug Development Corporation (DDC), and its objective would be to facilitate co-investment by government and private firms to increase the share of drug development financed by the public. To discharge its functions, the DDC would be structured as an independent, public, nonprofit corporation. The organization structure we recommend draws certain characteristics from that of the U.S. Postal Service, and others from the Independent System Operators (ISOs) that manage the interface between electric power generation and distribution.

A board of directors would be accountable for the operations of the DDC. Organizations such as the National Academy of Sciences, National Academy of Engineering, and the Institute of Medicine could recommend candidates for this board, with the secretary of health and human services and the president offering a slate of nominees for confirmation by the U.S. Senate. The DDC would comprise audit, arbitration, and other advisory committees.[2]

We are convinced that the independent corporation model is the best fit to ensure a continued steady stream of innovations in prescription pharmaceuticals. The DDC needs to be free from the kinds of day-to-day politics that can adversely influence the conduct of scientific research. It needs to be capable of operating in the marketplace with the flexibility of a private-sector organization while, at the same time, being accountable to oversight by both the legislative and executive branches of government.

Private research and development investments are significantly more profitable than other investments, and the returns to society are even greater.[3] To maintain social returns, the government has supported private research and development initiatives in several areas, especially for projects that otherwise could not be sustained by the private sector alone. The rationale for a DDC flows from the experience with these initiatives. For example, the Advanced Technology Program (ATP) was created in 1990 to directly fund private research and design to create social returns. The program was created by the Omnibus Trade and Competitiveness Act of 1988 and launched by President Bush with the goal of updating manufacturing technologies and funding research and discoveries that have the possibility of significant industrial benefits. Because of its focus on industry, ATP "is grounded in real-world needs." Companies present proposals to the ATP, with the intent of commercializing a discovery to which they will maintain all property rights if approved.

Choosing which projects to fund is a difficult process and, due to the large number of rejections, creates industrial tensions. Nonetheless, the program has been highly successful. Research has concluded that the ATP funds projects that otherwise would not have occurred privately, and that the social rate of return of these projects is considerable.[4] ATP also develops new information; half of ATP funded projects are granted a patent.[5]

Other examples of government supported technological programs exist. Directly funded initiatives such as ATP include the Small Business Innovation Research Program (SBIR Program) and SEMATECH. Programs that induce alliances between government and private scientists are Cooperative Research and Development Agreements (CRADAs), the Partnership for a New Generation of Vehicles (PNGV), and the Manufacturing Extension Partnership (MEP).[6]

## Reorganize the Pharmaceutical Industry

The second element of our solution is to "de-integrate" the pharmaceutical industry and separate drug discovery/development firms from manufacturing/distribution firms.

Organizations engaged in drug-development activity would be allowed to form collaborations and alliances with other players in the sector, because collaborations have been shown to be consistent with greater R & D productivity. These organizations would also be encouraged to conduct their operations in a manner that would take full advantage of economies of scale and scope that have been shown to benefit the process.[7] Results of all basic scientific studies and clinical trials would be expected to be submitted for publication in peer-reviewed journals as soon as patent and other intellectual property considerations permit. In the event that "negative" study results may not be deemed sufficiently significant to be published in major journals, they would be made a matter of the public record by the DDC.

To enforce the divestiture, the FDA would no longer accept applications for approval of new drugs from firms that continue to market drugs. The FDA's role in manufacturing and marketing drugs would remain unchanged. Mechanisms will need to be devised to ensure that international companies function according to the rules of this new U.S. market if they are to be approved for marketing in the United States.

Drug manufacturing/distribution firms might well modify their roles horizontally in a reorganized industry. As scientific progress leads to a family of new therapies for common disorders such as diabetes and asthma, whose effectiveness depends on patients' individual molecular characteristics, these firms might well offer multiple, targeted products within a given therapy area, and serve as sources of expertise in "disease management."[8]

Marketing firms would conduct so-called Phase IV testing. If additional indications can be found for drugs, then the marketing firm should benefit; it has brought new knowledge into the medical armamentarium. If adverse effects emerge, the marketing firm bears these risks as well, as it does today. As noted above, it will be considered a conflict of interest for a testing company to work for both types of companies at once.

Our solution could have been to impose on drug companies a reorganization along the lines of what economists call *atomistic competition*—an industry composed of a multitude of tiny firms. But this would not be an optimal industry organization for the marketing of new drugs. Such competition works well when products are stable and well known, but is problematic when new goods and services are introduced because demand for the new is unstable. Sewing machines long ago, and computers more recently, were new products that people had to learn how to work before they could use them properly and understand their value. Marketing activities by large firms facilitated their introduction. This initial uncertainty applies in spades to new drugs that may have a range of effects, both good and bad.

The history of drug innovation has shown the value of marketing new drugs, and this marketing is possible only if companies have sufficient market power to keep prices high enough to compensate them for these marketing expenses. Our solution is to license drug patents to the highest bidder in the hopes that this market power will encourage entry and marketing of new drugs without imposing the large costs on sick people that the current industry structure imposes.

## Set Drug Development Priorities

Priorities for drug development, as we argue in this book, need to be established based on impartial, objective assessments of medical and societal needs not only for the industrialized countries but also for the developing world. And within the industrialized countries that constitute the largest pharmaceutical markets, the needs of indigent, middle class, and wealthy populations need to be taken into account. The big challenge is how to accomplish this needs assessment in a manner that is not captured by special interests or the politics of the moment.

The process used by the NIH provides a model. For more than half a century, the NIH has managed to conduct research grant peer review successfully to distribute funding according to scientific merit, with minimal interference by special interests. The process is a two-stage review. The first stage is conducted by a group of professionals versed in scientific methods and analytical tools. This initial review group recommends a set of priorities. The results of this first review stage are then presented to another group, with broader representation from among recognized leaders in a range of fields, capable of making judgments that affect society as a whole.

This two-stage approach works partly because of incentives or constraints that operate on each stage. Reviewers in the first stage know another body will scrutinize their work. Second-stage reviewers find it difficult to "tamper" with recommendations that were based on scientific methods. The second group makes changes only to a small proportion of the initial recommendations.

Who would be engaged to conduct each of the two stages of the review under our solution? The first stage requires a multidisciplinary group that could collaborate to assemble and process the latest available data, which would include prevalence of illness and societal burden. Representation must include individuals knowledgeable in the natural and social sciences and medicine with experience in many domains of drug development and health care. First-stage reviewers could be drawn from the expert panels of the United States Pharmacopeia (USP), an organization discussed earlier in this book.

Second-stage reviewers would be drawn from recognized leaders broadly representative of society. We argue that the second stage should be managed by an organization comprised of distinguished scientists, and we propose to turn to the National Academy of Sciences (NAS), whose task forces today address problems well beyond purely scientific issues to embrace important science-based societal needs. The NAS would be fully capable of constituting the group that could suitably reconsider the recommendations of first-stage reviewers and develop a final list of priorities that determine the monetary rewards structure for those who successfully discover and develop needed medicines.

The NIH itself would be encouraged to continue and even enlarge its activities in drug discovery. The Bayh-Dole Act allowed scientists employed at NIH or supported by them to profit from the commercial application of their research. The act was designed to alter incentives for drug discovery, as does our solution. The new structure would enable scientists who are supported by public funds to profit from discoveries through the DDC auctions. While our solution does not explicitly alter anything in the NIH, it certainly is consistent with enlarging the NIH budget to encourage more drug development.

## Conduct Auctions

Auctions have become a tool of economic policy in the last decade, as countries have auctioned off the telecommunications spectrum for wireless communication. The experience of these auctions has been mixed. While some have been great successes, others have resulted in either low prices or troublesome litigation when successful bidders have defaulted on their commitments. Clearly, we would like to learn from this experience, but we believe that the auction model provides the best opportunity for a successful solution to the current problem of high drug prices.

In 1998, economist Michael Kremer suggested that auctions be used in the pharmaceutical industry.[9] Our solution is in the spirit of his proposal and follows his lead in some specifics as well. The major difference is that Kremer anticipated a process in which the government buys patents at auction and then places them in the public domain. The auction's purpose, therefore, would normally be only to reveal the market price, and the government would buy the patent at one of the high prices (it does not use the highest bid to avoid overvaluation). Our solution requires that *all* drug licenses be sold at auction to private companies in order to make the auction serious.

Under our solution, licenses for new drugs would be auctioned off by the DDC through a sealed-bid final auction, that is, by one-shot auctions where all firms submit single sealed bids. We expect these bids to be based on the present value of anticipated net profits to be earned from aggressive marketing of the drug. Companies may need to learn what these profits will be under the new industry configuration. There does not appear to be a way to short-circuit this process; we anticipate a period of learning no matter what kind of auction is used.

Clearly, setting up such a system entails a lot of uncertainty. If left unaided, the learning process might be so messy—resulting in high drug profits or failed auctions—that the DDC would be abandoned. To avoid this unhappy outcome, auctions must be designed to elicit information from drug firms and thus minimize the information burden on the DDC. One way to accomplish this would be for the DDC to call for two kinds of bids from drug marketing firms. Type 1 bids would be for an unrestricted license; Type 2 bids would be for a license with a price cap, or possibly even with a choice of more than one prospective price cap. Each company would be restricted to entering only one kind of bid.[10]

The first, unrestricted type of bid indicates the present value of a new drug under our current market system. It could form the basis for the payment to the drug-development firm that is offering the new drug for sale. The second type of bid shows what the drug is worth subject to a price cap. The higher the cap, the higher the price offered in the auction. The DDC will have to balance its mission to lower drug prices and its need to attract bidders of this second type. Asking marketing companies to bid for a menu of price caps is one way to elicit the needed information.

How would the DDC keep these bids honest? The DDC would announce that it would award drugs between the two kinds of bids randomly. It could announce, for example, that it would select a Type 1 bid with no price cap one-fourth of the time and a Type 2 bid with a price cap three-fourths of the time. The cost of this randomization is that one-fourth of new drugs would not have their prices lowered. The benefit would be that the DDC would acquire information about the market value of its drug licenses. As the DDC gained experience, it could begin to set the price caps from its prior experience and decrease the proportion of Type 1 bids it accepted.

The difference between the two kinds of bids is a measure of the present value of the revenue stream lost by the price cap. If the price cap is low, then the difference between the two kinds of bids will be large. The R & D firm is compensated from the first kind of bid, and the expense to the DDC rises with the severity of the price cap. Clearly a tradeoff exists between lowering drug prices drastically all at once and running a program at moderate cost. We anticipate that the DDC would begin by setting relatively modest price caps, first reducing prices by a small proportion. This would limit the DDC's exposure and minimize costs. Over time, the DDC could then set lower price limits if it was financially feasible.

Of course, any company bidding would have to worry about risks. One such risk is that a "me-too" drug would come along. This is the same risk drug companies face today when marketing medicines with unique properties. The market contest between Tagamet and Zantac is the best-known example of this problem. Bidding companies would bid with the risk that there might be a competitive drug and that it is price-controlled. Alternatively, if the first innovative drug were price controlled, then how would drug companies value a "me-too" drug with this low-priced competitor on the market? We believe that these risks are simply the risks of doing business today and should continue to be borne by the drug companies. Only time will tell how severe an impact these risks will have on the bidding process.

Patents of value are key to our solution, and good lawyers are needed to get valuable patents. Poorly skilled lawyers may apply for too narrow a patent or phrase the patent application loosely so that limitations are easily possible. Research and development companies should realize this and engage good lawyers. These high-powered helpers are expensive, but they will pay for themselves in the form of higher auction prices for patents. And if the companies have been able to finance drug discovery, this added expense should not strain their finances.

The payment for a drug would not be determined solely by the auction price. That price would be increased or decreased according to the value placed on the type of drug by the DDC as expressed by a publicly known multiplier. For example, the DDC might value drugs for tropical diseases more highly than the largely temperate American market. If so, the anticipation of greater returns from drug discovery might attract groups and firms to engage in the search for cures for tropical diseases. These groups and firms would choose to bear the risk because of the expected monetary return to their activities; the costs of risk would not be imposed on people suffering from tropical diseases.

But concerns remain with the establishment of auctions. As Paul Klemperer, a noted expert in the field of telecommunications auctions concluded, "What really matters in practical auction design is robustness against collusion and attractiveness of entry—just as in ordinary industrial markets." He tells the story of a German telephone auction with rules stating that sequential bids had to exceed previous bids by 10 percent. There were only two bidders: one company bid 20 million DM for half of the radio frequency spectrum and 18.18 million DM for the other; the other company took this as an offer to bid 20 million DM for the second half and divide the market at this low price. The offer was accepted, and the two companies walked away with cheap spectrum.[11]

This story illustrates the pitfalls to avoid. There should always be a multitude of bidders, never as few as two or three. And the auction process itself must not offer easy ways for the bidding companies to communicate. These guidelines may be easier to state than to implement, so the DDC will need the authority to modify its auction rules if the outcomes are not satisfactory. There was a lot of learning by doing in the telecommunications auctions, and we want to allow for similar learning in the pharmaceutical industry.

Entry is a harder issue. Clearly, companies that have a track record of drug marketing and sales will be eligible to bid. We want new companies to be able to enter this industry, but the DDC cannot allow just any firm to walk in off the street and bid an unrealistic amount for a license. That would only introduce confusion and litigation into the process. Under our solution, new entrants would be required to post a bond against their bid and put funds in escrow to place a bid. The funds would be returned to them after they demonstrate good faith in their bid, that is, after they make an initial sales offering.

It seems counterintuitive to encourage entry by placing an additional barrier to entry, but the bond would serve two purposes. First, it would assure the DDC that the bidder has the financial resources to market a drug. If a company is so starved for resources that it cannot even post a bond, it is in no position to break into the market for prescription drugs. We assume that capital would be available at reasonable cost for serious bidders. Second, the bond would provide a fund for the DDC to use if the bidder defaults in any way from the responsibilities of bidding for and marketing new drugs. This would prevent bidders who are not serious from imposing large costs on the DDC to clean up problems they create.

So, while the bond technically would be a barrier to entry in that it would discourage some bidders, it would only discourage spurious entry by companies whose aims are not really to enter the drug business. We believe that this simple device would, in fact, *encourage* entry by more serious companies. The barrier to them would not be large and they would be encouraged to make serious bids by the requirement to post and their desire to recover their bonds. This is, in a sense, a parallel to "managed competition" in health care more generally, where minimum requirements of health plans are required to ensure that contracts go to serious firms.[12]

This bond, therefore, would be a defense against the kinds of problems that are beginning to surface with another policy innovation—charter schools. The largest chain of publicly financed but privately run charter schools in California became insolvent and simply vanished as public schools opened for the year in the fall of 2004. Students were left without school records or schools to attend. Large burdens were thrust onto parents, school districts, and fired teachers as the charter schools suddenly disappeared. There was no way to force the charter school organization to share the costs or even to provide the normal reference functions of schools after students and teachers have gone.[13]

## *Avoid Collusion*

We recognize that collusion in the reorganized industry could be a problem under our solution, so the DDC and its rules not only have to avoid collusion among drug-distribution firms but also avoid collusion between distribution and discovery firms. There are two potential pitfalls. One is collusion among existing firms. The other is that one kind of firm enters the other's business, as is now happening in telecommunications as a result of the 1996 Telecommunications Act that blurred the distinction between local and long-distance service providers.[14] This migration could lead us back into the situation that our solution is designed to avoid.

It is instructive to review how this problem was handled in telecommunications and electric power where divestitures similar to our solution took place beginning in the 1980s. In 1982, the *Modification of Final Judgment*, an antitrust suit settlement agreement, required that AT&T divest itself of the Bell Operating Companies (BOC). AT&T, after divestiture, was allowed to act relatively freely; it was precluded, however, from "acquiring the stock or assets of any BOC." The BOCs and AT&T were large companies, so this provision was easy to enforce. The anticipation at the time of the divestiture was that AT&T would be stronger than the BOCs. As the telecommunications industry evolved, however, the regional BOCs emerged as far more powerful and aggressive than the divested AT&T. The restriction in the Modification of Final Judgment was honored, but it was hardly necessary.[15]

The story is similar in electric power. Vertically integrated, investor-owned utilities were broken up into separate generation and distribution companies. Most existing utilities retained their distribution networks and allowed the spun-off generator companies to deal with new entrants into electric power generation. The problem, more acute in electric power than in telecommunications, was to coordinate the newly independent generators and distributors, that is, to get the electricity from one to the other. This is achieved by means of the *electric grid*, a vast network of power lines that transports non-storable electricity. The grid, no longer the province of either divested set of companies, is now maintained by regional Independent Systems Operators (ISOs), who arrange for the transfer of electric power and maintenance of the network, and develop markets for the new intermediate products.

The learning curve in electric power was so great that it proved to be very costly, particularly to the people of California, and we want to avoid those kinds of costs here.[16] Under our solution, drug-discovery firms and drug-distribution firms would be precluded from having any explicit relations with each other—including a prohibition of stock or asset purchase. This was relevant in telecommunications over 20 years ago, but our prohibition would be broader to account for other forms of firm interactions. The two types of firms would be barred from having any joint ventures, prohibited from occupying the same physical premises, and no contractual arrangements between them would be permissible. The DDC, like the ISOs in the power industry, would monitor this interface.

Members of these various firms will continue to meet each other at professional gatherings and will continue to talk together. We cannot and do not want to proscribe informal professional contacts. It is imperative, though, that contractual relations of any type be avoided. Our solution requires, in the language of telecommunications long ago, that a "firewall" be built between the firms. The purpose of this prohibition is, of course, to point the drug discovery firms toward the auctions as their commercial goal and to have the drug-distribution firms in turn start from the auctions as they construct business plans.

## *Paying for Our Solution*

Under our solution, the federal government would need to assume the lion's share of private sector funding of drug development—around $30 billion annually, as discussed in earlier chapters. However, the actual commitment would not be that large, because it would be offset down the road by lower costs that the government would pay for the drugs themselves (for Medicare, Medicaid, and the

Veterans Administration and Department of Defense healthcare systems). Also, there would be substantial savings in transactions costs—lower costs of price negotiations and economic evaluations of the use of medicines.

Our solution would not magically make these billions of dollars disappear. It would, though, shift the burden of the expenditures from elderly and sick people to the overall population. In doing so, it would reduce the expenditures by aligning incentives to a public purpose. These gains are beneficial to both the citizens and the government of the United States.

To evaluate the transfers needed, let's compare them with the anticipated cost of Medicare Part D, described in Chapter 5, "How *Not* to Lower Drug Prices." The anticipated cost initially was $400 billion over 10 years, or $40 billion each year. It was clear from the start that this was a large underestimate of the cost of Medicare Part D, but let's use these figures to start. The FDA approves roughly 20 new chemical entities as new drugs each year, and we anticipate that this flow will not change drastically under our plan. The cost of a new drug, for which R & D firms should be compensated, has been estimated as approximately $1 billion. Although this includes capital costs and risks that will not be borne by the DDC under our solution, we use this cost as a starting point. If the DDC compensates drug discoverers at this rate, then the cost of our solution will be half the cost of Medicare Part D. This hypothetical cost also is close to the total estimated current size of pharmaceutical R & D of $30 billion.

The drug benefit funded by the government in Medicare Part D would become cheaper as drug prices fall. Other government drug programs, such as those implemented by the VA, would similarly find their costs falling. The savings resulting from these price cuts could be used to finance new drug discovery. In other words, as drug prices decline, the government's cost for Medicare would fall, freeing up resources for direct support of drug discovery. The DDC would not have to wait for these savings to be realized since it could predict the savings from the terms of its drug licenses. The two processes would develop concurrently. Let us assume, for example, that the restricted bids are subject to a 50 percent price reduction from what the market would bear without restrictions. The restricted bids, then, should be about half the size of unrestricted ones. The DDC and the marketing companies would thus share the cost of drug development equally (and, as we have noted, they would also share many of the risks).

Again, our solution includes a set of multipliers for drugs to off-set the difference between social benefit and commercial value. Drugs for tropical diseases are a prime example of drugs undervalued by the U.S. market. "Me-too" drugs may be candidates for drugs with commercial value in excess of their social value. We do not know how large the multipliers need to be to direct research and development; the DDC will have to learn from experience. Perhaps only a slight premium will be enough to stimulate R & D in these types of drugs. In any case, the DDC should start small and then evaluate the effects.

In this case, the DDC's activities could be financed completely by savings from Medicare Part D and other government programs. If Medicare Part D costs half of the projection, only $20 billion a year, this leaves $20 billion for the DDC to support drug R & D. Savings from the VA and other healthcare programs would add to the DDC's resources. With lower drug prices, the government would be able to transfer funds from support of the current pharmaceutical industry to support of drug R & D.

Of course, if drug prices were reduced below half their current price, then the savings from Medicare Part D would be greater. The need for resources to support R & D also would be larger, and the two can be expected to move in tandem. We do not want to reduce drug prices so much that Canadians take buses to Buffalo, New York, so that they can buy cheap drugs in the United States. So the program should start modestly.

The major part of these financial flows would go through the DDC. If we wanted to reduce the flow of funds through this new corporation, we could set the timing of the auctions earlier. There is a natural breaking point after Phase II trials, which furnish *proof of concept*—that is, they are the initial test of the efficacy of drugs for the indication studied. Phase III trials are confirmatory with larger samples. Almost all drugs that pass Phase II trials also pass Phase III trials, but a significant number fail at this point. Licenses auctioned after Phase II trials would, therefore, include drugs with "proof of concept" established, but some testing costs and risks would remain. Member firms in the manufacturing/distribution sector would be responsible for Phase III testing and submitting an NDA to the FDA. Auction prices, therefore, would incorporate both the risk that drugs might not gain FDA approval and the potential that the drug candidate could be the object of future development for additional drug indications.

Under this alternative plan, drug-distribution firms would bear some of the risk of drug development, but far less of the risk of drug discovery and development than at present. These companies would have obtained their drugs through auction, so most risks of discovery will not be their issue. The auction would be for drugs that have survived the "proof of concept" in Phase II tests. Only 20 percent of possible drug candidates survive to this stage; the development risks to this point would be borne by the discovery and development firms. Two-thirds of these drug candidates survive the remaining process of development, testing, and FDA approval to reach the market, and the licenses purchased from the DDC would still represent some development risk.

Since the auctions would take place earlier in the process of getting drugs to the market than the main plan, auction prices would be lower. Since marketing firms have more risk, they would pay less for the patent licenses. Development firms would receive less money as a result, but they would receive it earlier, they would no longer have to finance Phase III trials and the costs of winning FDA approval for New Drug Applications, and they would have slightly more putative drugs auctioned off. The DDC would have smaller financial flows coming through it as a result.

The problem with the earlier auctions is that marketing firms would be involved with Phase III trials and NDA approval. The pathologies of the current system described in earlier chapters would still be present. Setting the auctions earlier would, therefore, reduce the financial flows through the DDC at some cost to the purity of the new structure. Some of the ills we have observed today will not be addressed. It may nevertheless be desirable to move the auctions earlier if there are good reasons to do so.

This discussion has assumed that the rate of discovery of new drugs will continue at the same rate as in the recent past. This simple assumption might well be wrong, either because the technology of drug discovery is improving or because the reorganization of drug discovery entices more scientists into this field. If the number of new drugs falls, we would be very disappointed and seek to discover the cause. We do not expect that to happen. If the number of new drugs rises, the DDC would incur additional expenses. This is hardly a problem—for at least two reasons. First, we have made very conservative assumptions about the savings from lower drug prices and we think there is a margin where total government payments for drugs will fall even if the number of new drugs increases. Second, if our solution results in an accelerated rate of new drug discovery, then everyone would regard the extra DDC expenses as a worthwhile expenditure for our nation—and perhaps our world—to improve health.

## *Endnotes*

[1] Temin, 1987, *op. cit.* See also: Joskow, 2000, *op. cit.*

[2] United States Postal Service, Biographies of the Board of Governors. www.usps.com/communications/organization/bog.htm (accesed May 16, 2007);

New York Independent System Operator NYISO Organizational Chart. www.nyiso.com/org.html (accessed May 16, 2007); ISO New England Governance Structure. www.iso-ne.com/about_the_iso/governance.html (accessed May 16, 2007); California ISO Organizational Chart. www.caiso.com/ aboutus/orgcharts/ (accessed May 16, 2007).

[3] Cohen, Linda R. and Roger G. Noll. 1991. *The Technology Pork Barrel.* Washington, D.C.: The Brookings Institution, 17.

[4] Link and Scott, 2001, *op. cit.*

[5] See www.atp.nist.gov (accessed May 16, 2007) for details on the National Institute of Standards and Technology Advanced Technology Program.

[6] Stiglitz and Wallsten, 1999, *op. cit.*

[7] Cockburn and Henderson, 2001, *op. cit.* See also Henderson and Cockburn, 1996, *op. cit.*

[8] Finkelstein, S. N., A. J. Sinskey, and S. M. Cooper, 2002. The coming paradigm shift in pharmaceuticals. *PharmaGenomics,* September/October:26–28. See also: Sinskey, A. J., S. N. Finkelstein, and S. M. Cooper. 2002a. Getting to rational drug design—at last. *PharmaGenomics,* November/December:18–22.

[9] Kremer, M. 1998. Patent buyouts: a mechanism for encouraging innovation. *Quarterly Journal of Economics* 113:4, 1137–1167.

[10] We thank Paul Klemperer of Nuffield College, Oxford, for this suggestion.

[11] Klemperer, Paul. 2004. *Auctions: Theory and Practice.* Princeton, N.J.: Princeton University Press.

[12] Enthoven, 1978 and 1978a, *op. cit.*

[13] Dillon, S. 2004. Collapse of 60 charter schools leaves Californians scrambling. *New York Times,* September 17:A1.

[14] U.S. Senate, Committee on Commerce, Science, and Transportation. 2006. *Competition in the Telecommunications Industry; Hearings.* 108th Cong., 1st sess., January 14, 2003. Washington, D.C.: US GPO.

[15] Temin, 1987, *op. cit.*

[16] Joskow, 2000, *op. cit.*

# INDEX

Page numbers followed by *n* indicate terms in endnotes.

**FINANCIAL TIMES**

In an increasingly competitive world, it is quality
of thinking that gives an edge—an idea that opens new
doors, a technique that solves a problem, or an insight
that simply helps make sense of it all.

We work with leading authors in the various arenas
of business and finance to bring cutting-edge thinking
and best-learning practices to a global market.

It is our goal to create world-class print publications
and electronic products that give readers
knowledge and understanding that can then be
applied, whether studying or at work.

To find out more about our business
products, you can visit us at www.ftpress.com.